Collins

TREASURE HOUSE

Teacher's Guide 3
Comprehension Skills

Author: Abigail Steel

HarperCollins
PUBLISHERS
Since 1817

William Collins' dream of knowledge for all began with the publication of his first book in 1819.

A self-educated mill worker, he not only enriched millions of lives, but also founded a flourishing publishing house. Today, staying true to this spirit, Collins books are packed with inspiration, innovation and practical expertise. They place you at the centre of a world of possibility and give you exactly what you need to explore it.

Collins. Freedom to teach.

Published by Collins
An imprint of HarperCollins*Publishers*
The News Building
1 London Bridge Street
London
SE1 9GF

Browse the complete Collins catalogue at
www.collins.co.uk

© HarperCollins*Publishers* Limited 2017

10 9 8 7 6 5 4 3 2

ISBN 978-0-00-822292-5

British Library Cataloguing in Publication Data

A catalogue record for this publication is available from the British Library.

Publishing Director: Lee Newman
Publishing Manager: Helen Doran
Senior Editor: Hannah Dove
Project Manager: Emily Hooton
Author: Abigail Steel
Development Editor: Hannah Hirst-Dunton
Copy-editor: Trish Chapman
Proofreader: Tracy Thomas
Cover design and artwork: Amparo Barrera and Ken Vail Graphic Design
Internal design concept: Amparo Barrera
Typesetter: Jouve India Private Ltd
Illustrations: Alberto Saichann (Beehive Illustration)
Production Controller: Rachel Weaver

Printed and bound by CPI Group (UK) Ltd, Croydon, CR0 4YY

Acknowledgements

The publishers wish to thank the following for permission to reproduce content. Every effort has been made to trace copyright holders and to obtain their permission for the use of copyright materials. The publishers will gladly receive any information enabling them to rectify any error or omission at the first opportunity.

The Estate of Val Biro for an extract on page 6 from *Gumdrop has a Birthday* by Val Biro, Puffin, 1992, copyright © Val Biro; John Talbot for an extract on page 20 from *The Dragon's Cold* by John Talbot, text © 1986 John Talbot. Reproduced by permission of John Talbot; HarperCollins Publishers Ltd for the extract on page 23 from *The Selfish Giant* by Tanya Landman, copyright © 2016 Tanya Landman. Reproduced by permission of HarperCollins Publisher Ltd; Faber & Faber Ltd and HarperCollins Publishers for an extract on page 37 from 'Roger the Dog' by Ted Hughes, from *Collected Poems for Children* by Ted Hughes and *What is the Truth? A Farmyard Fable for the Young* by Ted Hughes, copyright © Ted Hughes, 1984, Faber and Faber Ltd. Reproduced by permission of Faber & Faber Ltd and HarperCollins Publishers; Penguin Random House for an extract and 2 illustrations on page 40 and 41 from *The Tale of Peter Rabbit* by Beatrix Potter, copyright © Frederick Warne & Co., 1902, 2002. Reproduced by permission of Frederick Warne & Co. www. peterrabbit.com; Egmont UK Ltd for an extract on page 44 from *The Owl Who Was Afraid of the Dark* by Jill Tomlinson. Text copyright © 1968 The Estate of Jill Tomlinson. Published by Egmont UK Ltd and used with permission; HarperCollins Publishers Ltd for the extract on pages 46-47 from *Air-Sea Rescue* by Chris Oxlade, copyright © 2013 Chris Oxlade; the extract on pages 52-53 from 'The Car Trip' published in *Something's Drastic* by Michael Rosen, copyright © 2007 Michael Rosen. Reproduced by permission of HarperCollins Publisher Ltd; Pearson Education Australia for an extract on page 55 from *The Gigantic Turnip Tug* by Lois Walker, pp.3-6, copyright © 2007, Pearson Australia. Reproduced with permission; and HarperCollins Publishers Ltd for the extract on pages 58-59 from *The House in the Forest* by Janet Foxley, copyright © 2013 Janet Foxley; the extract on pages 61-62 from *Spider McDrew and the Egyptians* by Alan Durant, copyright © 2007 Alan Durant; the extract on pages 64-65 from *Chocolate: From bean to bar* by Anita Ganeri, copyright © HarperCollins Publishers Ltd 2013; and the extract on page 67 from *The Green Hedgehog* by Celia Warren, copyright © 2013 Celia Warren. Reproduced by permission of HarperCollins Publisher Ltd.

In some instances we have been unable to trace the owners of copyright material and we would appreciate any information that would enable us to do so.

Contents

About Treasure House

Treasure House is a comprehensive and flexible bank of books and online resources for teaching the English curriculum. The Treasure House series offers two different pathways: one covering each English strand discretely (Skills Focus Pathway) and one integrating texts and the strands to create a programme of study (Integrated English Pathway). This Teacher's Guide is part of the Skills Focus Pathway.

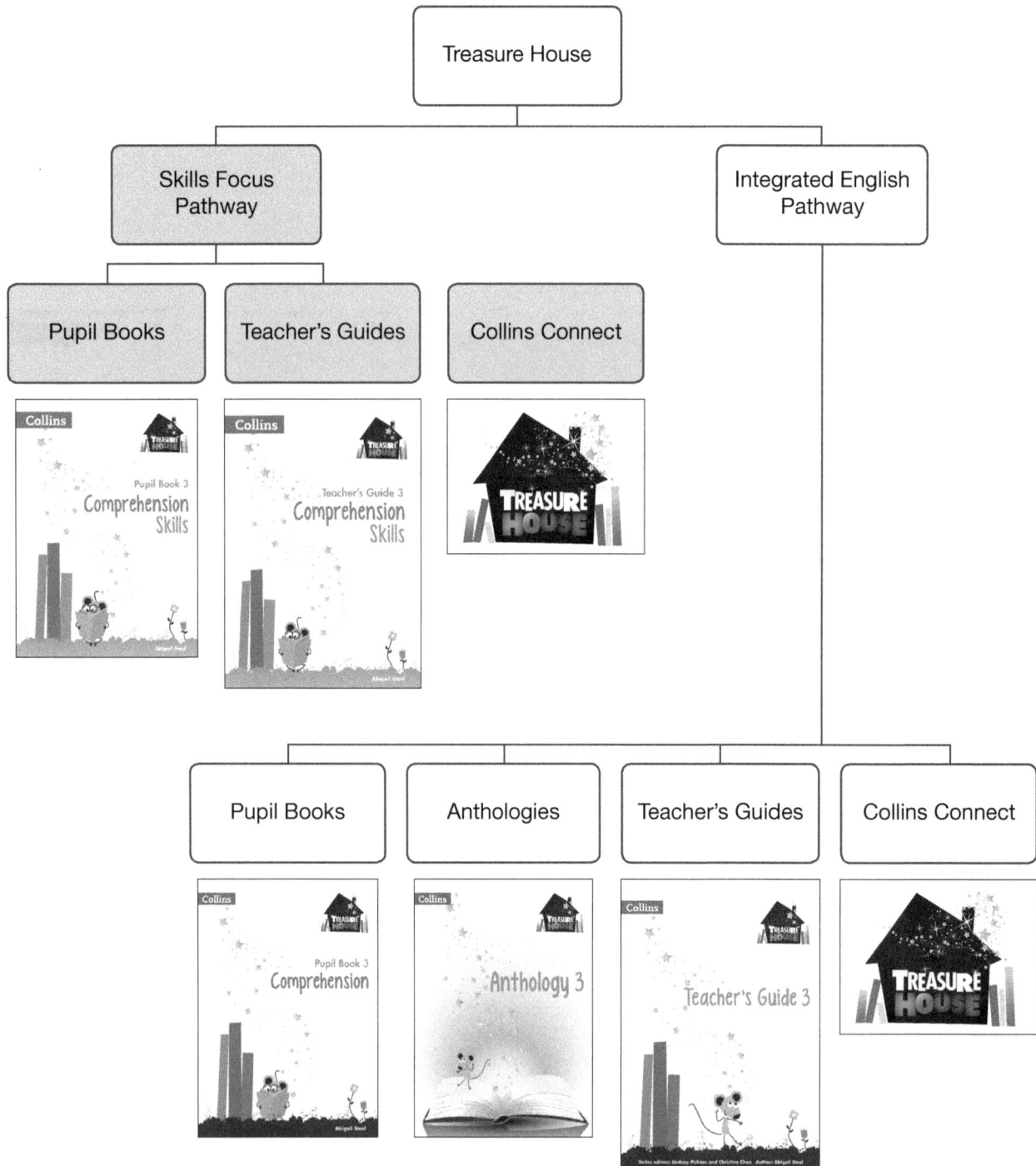

1. Skills Focus

The Skills Focus Pupil Books and Teacher's Guides for all four strands (Comprehension; Spelling; Composition; and Vocabulary, Grammar and Punctuation) allow you to teach each curriculum area in a targeted way. Each unit in the Pupil Book is mapped directly to the statutory requirements of the National Curriculum. Each Teacher's Guide provides step-by-step instructions to guide you through the Pupil Book activities and digital Collins Connect resources for each competency. With a clear focus on skills and clearly-listed curriculum objectives you can select the appropriate resources to support your lessons.

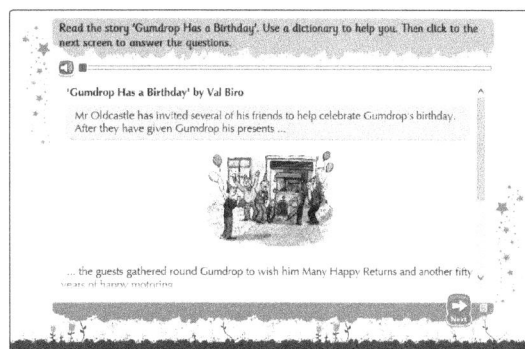

2. Integrated English

Alternatively, the Integrated English pathway offers a complete programme of genre-based teaching sequences. There is one Teacher's Guide and one Anthology for each year group. Each Teacher's Guide provides 15 teaching sequences focused on different genres of text such as fairy tales, letters and newspaper articles. The Anthologies contain the classic texts, fiction, non-fiction and poetry required for each sequence. Each sequence also weaves together all four dimensions of the National Curriculum for English – Comprehension; Spelling; Composition; and Vocabulary, Grammar and Punctuation – into a complete English programme. The Pupil Books and Collins Connect provide targeted explanation of key points and practice activities organised by strand. This programme provides 30 weeks of teaching inspiration.

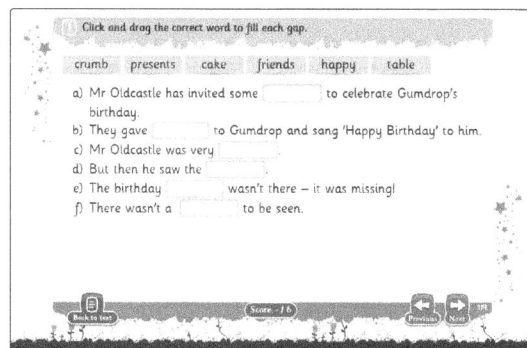

Other components

Handwriting Books, Handwriting Workbooks, Word Books and the online digital resources on Collins Connect are suitable for use with both pathways.

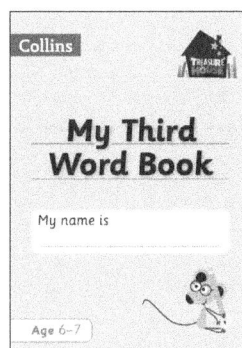

Treasure House Skills Focus Teacher's Guides

Year	Comprehension	Composition	Vocabulary, Grammar and Punctuation	Spelling
1	978-0-00-822290-1	978-0-00-822302-1	978-0-00-822296-3	978-0-00-822308-3
2	978-0-00-822291-8	978-0-00-822303-8	978-0-00-822297-0	978-0-00-822309-0
3	978-0-00-822292-5	978-0-00-822304-5	978-0-00-822298-7	978-0-00-822310-6
4	978-0-00-822293-2	978-0-00-822305-2	978-0-00-822299-4	978-0-00-822311-3
5	978-0-00-822294-9	978-0-00-822306-9	978-0-00-822300-7	978-0-00-822312-0
6	978-0-00-822295-6	978-0-00-822307-6	978-0-00-822301-4	978-0-00-822313-7

Inside the Skills Focus Teacher's Guides

The teaching notes in each unit in the Teacher's Guide provide you with subject information or background, a range of whole class and differentiated activities including photocopiable resource sheets and links to the Pupil Book and the online Collins Connect activities.

Each **Overview** provides clear objectives for each lesson tied into the new curriculum, links to the other relevant components and a list of any additional resources required.

Teaching overview provides a brief introduction to the specific skill concept or text type and some pointers on how to approach it.

Support, embed & challenge supports a mastery approach with activities provided at three levels.

Unit 2: Poetry: 'Caterpillars'

Overview

English curriculum objectives
- Listen to and discuss a wide range of fiction, poetry, plays, non-fiction and reference books or textbooks
- Read books that are structured in different ways and reading for a range of purposes
- Use dictionaries to check the meanings of words they have read
- Identify themes and conventions in a wide range of books
- Prepare poems and play scripts to read aloud and to perform, showing understanding through intonation, tone, volume and action
- Discuss words and phrases that capture the reader's interest and imagination
- Recognise some different forms of poetry
- Check that the text makes sense to them, discussing their understanding and explaining the meaning of words in context
- Ask questions to improve their understanding of a text

- Draw inferences such as inferring characters' feelings, thoughts and motives from their actions, and justifying inferences with evidence
- Identify how language, structure and presentation contribute to meaning
- Participate in discussion about both books that are read to them and those they can read for themselves, taking turns and listening to what others say

Treasure House resources
- Comprehension Skills Pupil Book 3, Unit 2, pages 7–8
- Collins Connect Treasure House Comprehension Year 3, Unit 2
- Photocopiable Unit 2, Resource 1: Similes, page 67
- Photocopiable Unit 2, Resource 2: My caterpillars poem, page 68

Additional resources
- Dictionaries or the internet (optional)
- Other poems about caterpillars (optional)

Introduction

Teaching overview

'Caterpillars' is a descriptive poem about a familiar creature. It describes its subject in a positive way and is effective at both portraying caterpillars and engaging the reader. The description is simple, rhythmic (four beats per line) and uses rhyming couplets.

Introduce the poem

Ask the children to talk in pairs, taking turns to describe a caterpillar. Ask them to talk about how caterpillars look and behave. Then ask each pair to share their ideas with the class.

Tell the children that, in this lesson, they will focus on a poem that describes caterpillars. Then they will answer questions about it. Remind them that sometimes the answers to the questions will be clearly written in the poem, but that sometimes they may need to think a little harder and use their own ideas, supported by the text.

Ask the children to read the poem individually or in pairs. Ask them to note down any words they do not understand. Discuss any unknown or unusual vocabulary before setting the children to work answering the questions in the Pupil Book. Try to avoid discussing the content of the poem until after the children have answered the questions.

Pupil practice

Get started

The children copy the sentences and complete them using information from the text.

Answers
1. Some have patches like polka dots [1 mark]
2. Clinging to twigs with tiny feet [1 mark]

Pupil Book pages 7–8

3. But mostly green like the leaves they chew. [1 mark]
4. Wiggling, woggling up and down [1 mark]
5. Always looking for something to eat. [1 mark]

Try these

Assist the children if they ask for help with vocabulary, first discussing what they think the words might mean. Ask them to write sentences to answer the questions, explaining their answers with reference to the text or their own experiences.

Suggested answers
1. According to the poem, not all caterpillars are green. They can also be brown, yellow or blue. [example]
2. Bristles are short, stiff hairs. [1 mark]
3. No, the caterpillars are not really painted. [1 mark] Explain that we call a comparison like this a simile.
4. The poet says the caterpillars are painted to describe how bright they are and to compare them with clowns (which really are painted). [1 mark]

5. 'Woggling' could be a cross between 'wiggling' and 'wobbling'. [1 mark]

Now try these
Open-ended questions
1. The children should note down at least three reasonable ideas for similes. [1 mark per simile]
2. Rhyming words: 'down'/'clown'; 'feet'/'eat'; 'spots'/'dots'; 'blue'/'chew'. [1 mark] The children should write two pairs of rhyming lines about the caterpillars. [4 marks]
3. Pictures should be relevant to the poem, including details it mentions. [3 marks]

Support, embed & challenge

Support

Use Unit 2 Resource 1: Similes to support the children in understanding the concept of a simile. Remind them of the line in the poem, 'Painted as bright as a circus clown', and point out that the caterpillars are compared to circus clowns. Explain that we call a comparison like this a simile. Show the children the resource sheet and read the first part of each simile aloud. Then read some of the possible words that could complete the simile and talk about which might constitute a suitable ending. Ask the children, possibly in pairs, to draw lines to complete the similes appropriately. (**Answers** as slow as a snail; as cold as ice; as busy as a bee; as blind as a bat; as light as a feather; as bright as the sun; as sweet as sugar; as playful as a kitten; as flat as a pancake; as hard as iron)

Embed

Use Unit 2 Resource 2: My caterpillars poem to encourage the children to apply their learning by writing their own extension to the 'Caterpillars' poem in the same style. Ask the children to continue the poem by writing more about the caterpillars. Suggest they use four pairs of rhyming lines, as Eric Slater's poem does. Remind them of the line in the poem, 'Painted as bright as a circus clown', and point out that the caterpillars are compared to circus clowns. Explain that we call a comparison like this a simile. Ask them to try to use one new simile in their new lines.

Challenge

Challenge the children to think about a different creature and the qualities it has. Ask them to make notes and/or a poem about the creature in the same style as 'Caterpillars'.

Homework / Additional activities

More about caterpillars

Ask children to research and find out five interesting facts about caterpillars that they can share with the class.

Collins Connect: Unit 2

Ask the children to complete Unit 2 (see Teach → Year 3 → Comprehension → Unit 2).

Introduce the concept/text provides 5–10 minutes of preliminary discussion points or class/group activities to get the pupils engaged in the lesson focus and set out any essential prior learning.

Pupil practice gives guidance and the answers to each of the three sections in the Pupil Book: *Get started*, *Try these* and *Now try these*.

Homework / Additional activities lists ideas for classroom or homework activities, and relevant activities from Collins Connect.

Two photocopiable **resource** worksheets per unit provide extra practice of the specific lesson concept. They are designed to be used with the activities in support, embed or challenge sections.

Unit 2 Resource 1
Similes

A simile compares one thing to another thing. Similes usually use 'as' or 'like' to compare the two things.

For example: 'Painted as bright as a circus clown'.

Draw lines to complete the similes by making good comparisons.

as slow as…	ice
as cold as…	a kitten
as busy as…	sugar
as blind as…	a bat
as light as…	a pancake
as bright as…	a snail
as sweet as…	iron
as playful as…	the sun
as flat as…	a feather
as hard as…	a bee

Unit 2 Resource 2
My caterpillars poem

Continue the poem by writing more about the caterpillars. Use four pairs of rhyming lines, as the 'Caterpillars' poem does. Try to use one new simile in your poem.

Simile ideas
as smooth as silk
as bristly as a toothbrush
as hungry as a horse
as green as grass

My ideas for rhyming words

Caterpillars

By _____

Treasure House Skills Focus Pupil Books

There are four Skills Focus Pupil Books for each year group, based on the four dimensions of the National Curriculum for English: Comprehension; Spelling; Composition; and Vocabulary, Grammar and Punctuation. The Pupil Books provide a child-friendly introduction to each subject and a range of initial activities for independent pupil-led learning. A Review unit for each term assesses pupils' progress.

Year	Comprehension	Composition	Vocabulary, Grammar and Punctuation	Spelling
1	978-0-00-823634-2	978-0-00-823646-5	978-0-00-823640-3	978-0-00-823652-6
2	978-0-00-823635-9	978-0-00-823647-2	978-0-00-823641-0	978-0-00-823653-3
3	978-0-00-823636-6	978-0-00-823648-9	978-0-00-823642-7	978-0-00-823654-0
4	978-0-00-823637-3	978-0-00-823649-6	978-0-00-823643-4	978-0-00-823655-7
5	978-0-00-823638-0	978-0-00-823650-2	978-0-00-823644-1	978-0-00-823656-4
6	978-0-00-823639-7	978-0-00-823651-9	978-0-00-823645-8	978-0-00-823657-1

Inside the Skills Focus Pupil Books

Comprehension

Includes high-quality text extracts covering poetry, prose, traditional tales, playscripts and non-fiction.

Pupils retrieve and record information, learn to draw inferences from texts and increase their familiarity with a wide range of literary genres.

Composition

Includes high-quality, annotated text extracts as models for different types of writing.

Children learn how to write effectively and for a purpose.

Vocabulary, Grammar and Punctuation

Develops children's knowledge and understanding of grammar and punctuation skills.

A rule is introduced and explained. Children are given lots of opportunities to practise using it.

Spelling

Spelling rules are introduced and explained.

Practice is provided for spotting and using the spelling rules, correcting misspelt words and using the words in context.

Treasure House on Collins Connect

Digital resources for Treasure House are available on Collins Connect which provides a wealth of interactive activities. Treasure House is organised into six core areas on Collins Connect:

- Comprehension
- Spelling
- Composition
- Vocabulary, Grammar and Punctuation
- The Reading Attic
- Teacher's Guides and Anthologies.

For most units in the Skills Focus Pupil Books, there is an accompanying Collins Connect unit focused on the same teaching objective. These fun, independent activities can be used for initial pupil-led learning, or for further practice using a different learning environment. Either way, with Collins Connect, you have a wealth of questions to help children embed their learning.

Treasure House on Collins Connect is available via subscription at connect.collins.co.uk

Features of Treasure House on Collins Connect

The digital resources enhance children's comprehension, spelling, composition, and vocabulary, grammar, punctuation skills through providing:

- a bank of varied and engaging interactive activities so children can practise their skills independently
- audio support to help children access the texts and activities
- auto-mark functionality so children receive instant feedback and have the opportunity to repeat tasks.

Teachers benefit from useful resources and time-saving tools including:

- teacher-facing materials such as audio and explanations for front-of-class teaching or pupil-led learning
- lesson starter videos for some Composition units
- downloadable teaching notes for all online activities
- downloadable teaching notes for Skills Focus and Integrated English pathways
- the option to assign homework activities to your classes
- class records to monitor progress.

Comprehension

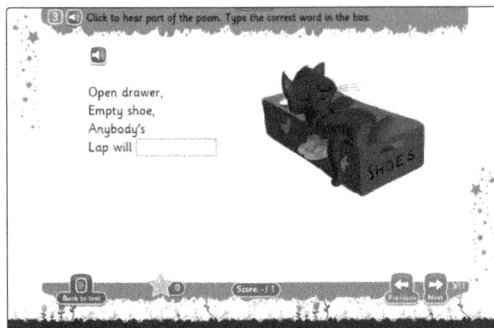

- Includes high-quality text extracts covering poetry, prose, traditional tales, playscripts and non-fiction.
- Audio function supports children to access the text and the activities

Composition

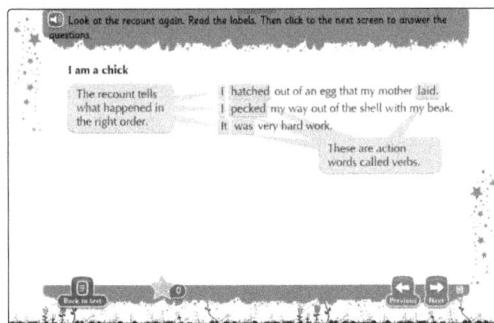

- Activities support children to develop and build more sophisticated sentence structures.
- Every unit ends with a longer piece of writing that can be submitted to the teacher for marking.

Vocabulary, Grammar and Punctuation

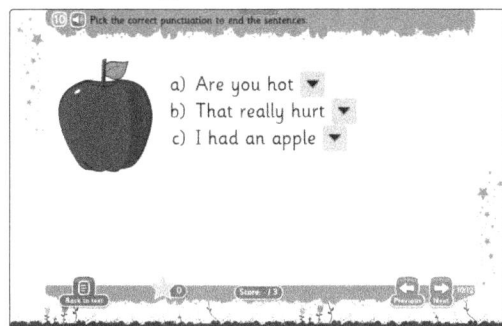

- Fun, practical activities develop children's knowledge and understanding of grammar and punctuation skills.
- Each skill is reinforced with a huge, varied bank of practice questions.

Spelling

- Fun, practical activities develop children's knowledge and understanding of each spelling rule.
- Each rule is reinforced with a huge, varied bank of practice questions.
- Children spell words using an audio prompt, write their own sentences and practise spelling using Look Say Cover Write Check.

Reading Attic

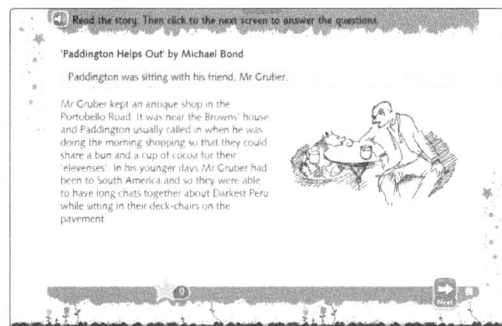

- Children's love of reading is nurtured with texts from exciting children's authors including Micheal Bond, David Walliams and Micheal Morpurgo.
- Lesson sequences accompany the texts, with drama opportunities and creative strategies for engaging children with key themes, characters and plots.
- Whole-book projects encourage reading for pleasure.

Treasure House Digital Teacher's Guides and Anthologies

The teaching sequences and anthology texts for each year group are included as a flexible bank of resources.

The teaching notes for each skill strand and year group are also included on Collins Connect.

Support, embed and challenge

Treasure House provides comprehensive, detailed differentiation at three levels to ensure that all children are able to access achievement. It is important that children master the basic skills before they go further in their learning. Children may make progress towards the standard at different speeds, with some not reaching it until the very end of the year.

In the Teacher's Guide, Support, Embed and Challenge sections allow teachers to keep the whole class focussed with no child left behind. Two photocopiable resources per unit offer additional material linked to the Support, Embed or Challenge sections.

Support

The Support section offers simpler or more scaffolded activities that will help learners who have not yet grasped specific concepts covered. Background information may also be provided to help children to contextualise learning. This enables children to make progress so that they can keep up with the class.

To help with reading comprehension, some support activities help learners to access the core text, for example, by giving some background information to the story or support with figurative speech. This is more motivating and enjoyable than offering a simplified text.

If you have a teaching assistant, you may wish to ask him or her to help children work through these activities. You might then ask children who have completed these activities to progress to other more challenging tasks found in the Embed or Challenge sections – or you may decide more practice of the basics is required. Collins Connect can provide further activities.

Embed

The Embed section includes activities to embed learning and is aimed at those who children who are working at the expected standard. It ensures that learners have understood key teaching objectives for the age-group. These activities could be used by the whole class or groups, and most are appropriate for both teacher-led and independent work.

In Comprehension, all children should cross the threshold of reading the texts in Treasure House; however, the depth of their analysis and understanding will vary depending on prior experience, current interests and motivation. Activities in the Embed section encourage children to apply their learning by further analysing the text or by planning their own writing based on the same theme or text-type.

Challenge

The Challenge section provides additional tasks, questions or activities that will push children who have mastered the concept without difficulty. This keeps children motivated and allows them to gain a greater depth of understanding. You may wish to give these activities to fast finishers to work through independently.

In Comprehension, children explore the text-type or theme further through drama, research, discussion or by doing their own writing.

Assessment

Teacher's Guides

There are opportunities for assessment throughout the Treasure House series. The teaching notes in Treasure House Teacher's Guides offer ideas for questions, informal assessment and spelling tests.

Pupil Book Review units

Each Pupil Book has three Review units designed as a quick formative assessment tool for the end of each term. Questions assess the work that has been covered over the previous units. These review units will provide you with an informal way of measuring your pupils' progress. You may wish to use these as Assessment for Learning to help you and your pupils to understand where they are in their learning journey.

The Review units in the Comprehension Pupil Books provide children with a new text or extract to read and understand. Children can draw on what they have learned during the term to help them access the new text without an initial teaching session to guide them. Questions types may reoccur across the Review units allowing you to see progression across the year, and the three reviews will always cover all three genres: fiction, non-fiction and poetry.

Assessment in Collins Connect

Activities on Collins Connect can also be used for effective assessment. Activities with auto-marking mean that if children answer incorrectly, they can make another attempt helping them to analyse their own work for mistakes. Homework activities can also be assigned to classes through Collins Connect. At the end of activities, children can select a smiley face to indicate how they found the task giving you useful feedback on any gaps in knowledge.

Class records on Collins Connect allow you to get an overview of children's progress with several features. You can choose to view records by unit, pupil or strand. By viewing detailed scores, you can view pupils' scores question by question in a clear table-format to help you establish areas where there might be particular strengths and weaknesses both class-wide and for individuals.

If you wish, you can also set mastery judgements (mastery achieved and exceeded, mastery achieved, mastery not yet achieved) to help see where your children need more help.

Support with teaching comprehension

The teacher's guides for Comprehension units can be followed in a simple linear fashion that structures the lesson into five sections:

- assessment of existing skills and knowledge, and an introduction to the unit's source text
- reading the source text
- completion of the 'pupil practice' questions
- differentiated work, following the Support, Embed and Challenge activity guidance (using the provided photocopiable worksheets)
- homework or additional activities.

However, this lesson structure is intended to be flexible. While we recommend that the first three of these steps should usually be followed in the given order, work following the pupil practice questions can be manipulated in numerous ways to suit the needs, skills and preferences of your class.

For example, you may wish to set one of the differentiation activities as homework for the whole class, or to guide children through an 'additional' activity during the lesson, rather than setting it as homework. You may alternatively judge that your class has firmly grasped the concept being taught, and choose not to use any activity suggested, or perhaps introduce only the Extend activity: it is not essential that every activity outlined in the teacher's guide units should be completed.

With the same motivation, many activities (and worksheets) could be adapted for reuse in units other than the one for which they are provided. Several activity and worksheet types are already repeated in similar forms between (and sometimes within) year groups. This is in order both to show the children's changing levels of attainment directly, and to allow any children who have found an activity challenging to reattempt it in a new context after developing their skills.

If, however, children find a particular activity either challenging or particularly engaging, you should also feel free to repeat that activity, where appropriate, at your own discretion. For example, if children enjoy considering appropriate costumes and settings when looking at a playscript (an activity, with worksheet, suggested in Year 3 Unit 17), this activity could be adapted to fit any playscript source text – and many prose fiction texts, too.

You may also wish to consider using Support activities in conjunction with the pupil practice questions, if children are struggling with content or a concept with which the Support activity deals. For example, if questions within the 'Try these' and 'Now try these' sections of pupil practice require understanding of similes, you may wish to intervene and prepare children using an appropriate Support activity (such as suggested in Year 3 Unit 2).

By using the teacher's guide units and their suggested activities flexibly, you can choose to tailor the resources at your fingertips to provide the most beneficial learning system for the children being taught.

Teaching comprehension is a key part of achieving the universal aim of developing children's love of literature through widespread reading for enjoyment. If children are confident and fluent readers, who understand the form and content of the texts they read they are more likely to enjoy them.

We can make learning comprehension easy and fun by employing simple techniques to guide children along their reading journey.

Modelling

When reading a letter or newspaper article to the class remember to hesitate on words that they might not know, intimate that you are unsure of the proper meaning and look them up in a dictionary. You might also model how you use context or grammar clues to work out the meaning using the rest of the text.

Making predictions

When embarking on any new text ask children to consider what they think it will be about, or what they think might happen. Show how to look for clues in the presentation of the text or the introductory information you have. Remember to model making your own predictions too – this gives you an opportunity to demonstrate how to rationalize a prediction by speaking your thought processes aloud.

Questioning

Questioning can take many forms and penetrate many depths of understanding. Questions can be closed, requiring short, defined answers or they can be open, enabling the children to explore wider thoughts. Sometimes the best questions are those that are spontaneous and form part of a natural conversation exploring a text. Encourage children to form their own questions about the purpose, structure and content of texts – they could note these down and return to them later to see if they have discovered the answers after reading.

Retelling and summarizing

Encourage children to reflect upon what has happened in a text – this can be a surprisingly challenging activity. Provide plenty of demonstrations of how to retell and summarize. Retelling and summarizing can take many fun, interactive forms such as role play, radio presentations, creating news flash articles, and oral story retellings. Some children struggle with sequencing and ordering so build this in with your retelling activities.

Visualizing

When we read we create mental images of what is happening. Descriptions of people, places and action are acted out in our minds. For children this skill doesn't always come naturally. Ask children to close their eyes and focus on imagining how something looks. Compare written texts to the films and TV shows they are familiar with watching. Point out specific adjectives and adverbs that are actively working within the text to assist the reader. Enable children the opportunity to draw and paint their interpretations of the texts they read.

Connections to children's own experiences

Younger children are often better at pointing at when they recognise a similarity between their own life and something they read in a text. Older children tend to become less inward looking and aren't so forthcoming with the links they make to texts. Encourage them by asking direct questions: *Does anyone else recognise this event? Do you know a character like this? Have you ever been to a similar place? When have you felt that emotion like the character?* Making explicit connections with the text can advance children's understanding of not only the event being described but also the history to the event and the character's emotions. They are able to talk about the 'bigger picture'.

Delivering the 2014 National Curriculum for English

English Programme of Study

Reading – comprehension

		Units																		
		1	2	3	4	5	6	7	8	9	10	11	12	13	14	15	16	17	18	19	20
Develop positive attitudes to reading and understanding of what they read by:	Listening to and discussing a wide range of fiction, poetry, plays, non-fiction and reference books or textbooks	✓	✓	✓	✓	✓	✓	✓	✓	✓	✓	✓	✓	✓	✓	✓	✓	✓	✓	✓	✓
	Reading books that are structured in different ways and reading for a range of purposes	✓	✓	✓	✓	✓	✓	✓	✓	✓	✓	✓	✓	✓	✓	✓	✓	✓	✓	✓	✓
	Using dictionaries to check the meaning of words that they have read	✓	✓	✓	✓	✓	✓	✓	✓	✓	✓	✓	✓	✓	✓	✓	✓	✓	✓	✓	✓
	Increasing their familiarity with a wide range of books, including fairy stories, myths and legends, and retelling some of these orally	✓				✓		✓						✓	✓			✓		✓	
	Identifying themes and conventions in a wide range of books	✓	✓	✓	✓	✓	✓	✓	✓	✓	✓	✓	✓	✓	✓	✓	✓	✓	✓	✓	✓
	Preparing poems and play scripts to read aloud and to perform, showing understanding through intonation, tone, volume and action												✓				✓	✓			
	Discussing words and phrases that capture the reader's interest and imagination	✓	✓	✓	✓	✓	✓	✓	✓	✓	✓	✓	✓	✓	✓	✓	✓	✓	✓	✓	✓
	Recognising some different forms of poetry [for example, free verse, narrative poetry]		✓	✓													✓				

English Programme of Study

Reading – comprehension

Reading – comprehension	1	2	3	4	5	6	7	8	9	10	11	12	13	14	15	16	17	18	19	20
Understand what they read, in books they can read independently, by: Checking that the text makes sense to them, discussing their understanding and explaining the meaning of words in context	✓	✓	✓	✓	✓	✓	✓	✓	✓	✓	✓	✓	✓	✓	✓	✓	✓	✓	✓	✓
Asking questions to improve their understanding of a text	✓	✓	✓	✓	✓	✓	✓	✓	✓	✓	✓	✓	✓	✓	✓	✓	✓	✓	✓	✓
Drawing inferences such as inferring characters' feelings, thoughts and motives from their actions, and justifying inferences with evidence	✓	✓		✓	✓	✓	✓	✓	✓	✓	✓	✓	✓	✓	✓	✓	✓	✓	✓	✓
Predicting what might happen from details stated and implied	✓				✓	✓	✓	✓	✓	✓	✓		✓	✓			✓	✓	✓	✓
Identifying main ideas drawn from more than one paragraph and summarising these	✓			✓	✓	✓	✓	✓	✓	✓	✓	✓	✓	✓	✓		✓	✓	✓	✓
Identifying how language, structure, and presentation contribute to meaning	✓	✓	✓	✓	✓	✓	✓	✓	✓	✓	✓	✓	✓	✓		✓	✓	✓	✓	✓
Retrieve and record information from non-fiction									✓	✓	✓				✓			✓	✓	✓
Participate in discussion about both books that are read to them and those they can read for themselves, taking turns and listening to what others say.	✓	✓	✓	✓	✓	✓	✓	✓	✓	✓	✓	✓	✓	✓	✓	✓	✓	✓	✓	✓

Treasure House resources overview

Unit	Title	Treasure House Resources	Collins Connect

1	Fiction: 'Gumdrop has a Birthday'	• Comprehension Skills Pupil Book 3, Unit 1, pages 4–6
		• Comprehension Skills Teacher's Guide 3
		  – Unit 1, pages 22–23
		  – Photocopiable Unit 1, Resource 1: Ordering events, page 65
		  – Photocopiable Unit 1, Resource 2: A thank-you letter, page 66
			Collins Connect Treasure House Comprehension Year 3, Unit 1

2	Poetry: 'Caterpillars'	• Comprehension Skills Pupil Book 3, Unit 2, pages 7–8
		• Comprehension Skills Teacher's Guide 3
		  – Unit 2, pages 24–25
		  – Photocopiable Unit 2, Resource 1: Similes, page 67
		  – Photocopiable Unit 2, Resource 2: My caterpillars poem, page 68
			Collins Connect Treasure House Comprehension Year 3, Unit 2

3	Poetry: 'The Cow'	• Comprehension Skills Pupil Book 3, Unit 3, pages 9–10
		• Comprehension Skills Teacher's Guide 3
		  – Unit 3, pages 26–27
		  – Photocopiable Unit 3, Resource 1: Comparing animals, page 69
		  – Photocopiable Unit 3, Resource 2: My animal poem, page 70
			Collins Connect Treasure House Comprehension Year 3, Unit 3

4	Non-fiction (news report): 'Monkey Business'	• Comprehension Skills Pupil Book 3, Unit 4, pages 11–13
		• Comprehension Skills Teacher's Guide 3
		  – Unit 4, pages 28–29
		  – Photocopiable Unit 4, Resource 1: Find the facts, page 71
		  – Photocopiable Unit 4, Resource 2: A new news report, page 72
			Collins Connect Treasure House Comprehension Year 3, Unit 4

5	Fiction (traditional story) 'Thunder and Lightning'	• Comprehension Skills Pupil Book 3, Unit 5, pages 14–16
		• Comprehension Skills Teacher's Guide 3
		  – Unit 5, pages 30–31
		  – Photocopiable Unit 5, Resource 1: Retell the tale, page 73
		  – Photocopiable Unit 5, Resource 2: The tale of Rain, page 74
			Collins Connect Treasure House Comprehension Year 3, Unit 5

6	Fiction (fable): 'The Lion and the Mouse'	• Comprehension Skills Pupil Book 3, Unit 6, pages 17–19
		• Comprehension Skills Teacher's Guide 3
		  – Unit 6, pages 32–33
		  – Photocopiable Unit 6, Resource 1: Making decisions, page 75
		  – Photocopiable Unit 6, Resource 2: Another moral tale, page 76
			Collins Connect Treasure House Comprehension Year 3, Unit 6

Unit	Title	Treasure House Resources	Collins Connect
7	Fiction: 'The Dragon's Cold'	• Comprehension Skills Pupil Book 3, Unit 7, pages 20–22 • Comprehension Skills Teacher's Guide 3 – Unit 7, pages 34–35 – Photocopiable Unit 7, Resource 1: Before and after, page 77 – Photocopiable Unit 7, Resource 2: How Duncan caught a cold, page 78	Collins Connect Treasure House Comprehension Year 3, Unit 7
8	Non-fiction (letter): 'Gran's New House'	• Comprehension Skills Pupil Book 3, Unit 8, pages 25–27 • Comprehension Skills Teacher's Guide 3 – Unit 8, pages 37–38 – Photocopiable Unit 8, Resource 1: Asking questions, page 79 – Photocopiable Unit 8, Resource 2: A letter home, page 80	Collins Connect Treasure House Comprehension Year 3, Unit 8
9	Non-fiction (information text): 'Ants'	• Comprehension Skills Pupil Book 3, Unit 9, pages 28–30 • Comprehension Skills Teacher's Guide 3 – Unit 9, pages 39–40 – Photocopiable Unit 9, Resource 1: Quick quiz, page 81 – Photocopiable Unit 9, Resource 2: Insect fact file, page 82	Collins Connect Treasure House Comprehension Year 3, Unit 9
10	Non-fiction (information text): 'On Holiday'	• Comprehension Skills Pupil Book 3, Unit 10, pages 31–33 • Comprehension Skills Teacher's Guide 3 – Unit 10, pages 41–42 – Photocopiable Unit 10, Resource 1: A letter of complaint, page 83 – Photocopiable Unit 10, Resource 2: Information pack, page 84	Collins Connect Treasure House Comprehension Year 3, Unit 10
11	Non-fiction (poster): 'Fun on Bikes'	• Comprehension Skills Pupil Book 3, Unit 11, pages 34–36 • Comprehension Skills Teacher's Guide 3 – Unit 11, pages 43–44 – Photocopiable Unit 11, Resource 1: The bike competition, page 85 – Photocopiable Unit 11, Resource 2: New event poster, page 86	Collins Connect Treasure House Comprehension Year 3, Unit 11
12	Poetry: 'Roger the Dog'	• Comprehension Skills Pupil Book 3, Unit 12, pages 37–39 • Comprehension Skills Teacher's Guide 3 – Unit 12, pages 45–46 – Photocopiable Unit 12, Resource 1: Rhyming words, page 87 – Photocopiable Unit 12, Resource 2: A new pet poem, page 88	Collins Connect Treasure House Comprehension Year 3, Unit 12

Unit	Title	Treasure House Resources	Collins Connect
13	Fiction (classic): 'The Tale of Peter Rabbit'	• Comprehension Skills Pupil Book 3, Unit 13, pages 40–42 • Comprehension Skills Teacher's Guide 3 – Unit 13, pages 47–48 – Photocopiable Unit 13, Resource 1: What was Peter thinking? page 89 – Photocopiable Unit 13, Resource 2: Peter in trouble, page 90	Collins Connect Treasure House Comprehension Year 3, Unit 13
14	Fiction (classic): 'The Owl Who Was Afraid of the Dark'	• Comprehension Skills Pupil Book 3, Unit 14, pages 43–45 • Comprehension Skills Teacher's Guide 3 – Unit 14, pages 49–50 – Photocopiable Unit 14, Resource 1: A 'proper' owl, page 91 – Photocopiable Unit 14, Resource 2: What happens next? page 92	Collins Connect Treasure House Comprehension Year 3, Unit 14
15	Non-fiction (information text): 'Funny Feeders'	• Comprehension Skills Pupil Book 3, Unit 15, pages 49–51 • Comprehension Skills Teacher's Guide 3 – Unit 15, pages 52–53 – Photocopiable Unit 15, Resource 1: True or false? page 93 – Photocopiable Unit 15, Resource 2: Information leaflet, page 94	Collins Connect Treasure House Comprehension Year 3, Unit 15
16	Poetry: 'The Car Trip'	• Comprehension Skills Pupil Book 3, Unit 16, pages 52–54 • Comprehension Skills Teacher's Guide 3 – Unit 16, pages 54–55 – Photocopiable Unit 16, Resource 1: The car-trip story, page 95 – Photocopiable Unit 16, Resource 2: Mum's view, page 96	
17	Playscript: 'The Gigantic Turnip Tug'	• Comprehension Skills Pupil Book 3, Unit 17, pages 55–57 • Comprehension Skills Teacher's Guide 3 – Unit 17, pages 56–57 – Photocopiable Unit 17, Resource 1: Finding the features, page 97 – Photocopiable Unit 17, Resource 2: Costumes and setting, page 98	
18	Fiction (traditional tale): 'The House in the Forest'	• Comprehension Skills Pupil Book 3, Unit 18, pages 58–60 • Comprehension Skills Teacher's Guide 3 – Unit 18, pages 58–59 – Photocopiable Unit 18, Resource 1: Helga's character, page 99 – Photocopiable Unit 18, Resource 2: Two diaries, page 100	

Unit	Title	Treasure House Resources	Collins Connect
19	Fiction (modern): 'Spider McDrew and the Egyptians'	• Comprehension Skills Pupil Book 3, Unit 19, pages 61–63 • Comprehension Skills Teacher's Guide 3 – Unit 19, pages 60–61 – Photocopiable Unit 19, Resource 1: Romans and Egyptians, page 101 – Photocopiable Unit 19, Resource 2: Spider's character, page 102	
20	Non-fiction (information text): 'Chocolate: From bean to bar'	• Comprehension Skills Pupil Book 3, Unit 20, pages 64–66 • Comprehension Skills Teacher's Guide 3 – Unit 20, pages 62–63 – Photocopiable Unit 20, Resource 1: True or false? page 103 – Photocopiable Unit 20, Resource 2: Food fact file, page 104	

Unit 1: Fiction: 'Gumdrop has a Birthday'

Overview

English curriculum objectives

- Listen to and discuss a wide range of fiction, poetry, plays, non-fiction and reference books or textbooks
- Read books that are structured in different ways and reading for a range of purposes
- Use dictionaries to check the meanings of words they have read
- Increase their familiarity with a wide range of books, including fairy stories, myths and legends, and retell some of these orally
- Identify themes and conventions in a wide range of books
- Discuss words and phrases that capture the reader's interest and imagination
- Check that the text makes sense to them, discussing their understanding and explaining the meaning of words in context
- Ask questions to improve their understanding of a text
- Draw inferences such as inferring characters' feelings, thoughts and motives from their actions, and justifying inferences with evidence

- Predict what might happen from details stated and implied
- Identify main ideas drawn from more than one paragraph and summarise these
- Identify how language, structure and presentation contribute to meaning
- Participate in discussion about both books that are read to them and those they can read for themselves, taking turns and listening to what others say

Treasure House resources

- Comprehension Skills Pupil Book 3, Unit 1, pages 4–6
- Collins Connect Treasure House Comprehension Year 3, Unit 1
- Photocopiable Unit 1, Resource 1: Ordering events, page 65
- Photocopiable Unit 1, Resource 2: A thank-you letter, page 66

Additional resources

- Dictionaries or the internet (optional)
- *Gumdrop has a Birthday* by Val Biro, whole text (optional)

Introduction

Teaching overview

Gumdrop has a Birthday tells the story of a birthday party Mr Oldcastle has thrown for Gumdrop, his beloved classic car. His friends are looking forward to the birthday cake, but it seems to have vanished – and Horace the dog is looking very fat and happy.

Introduce the extract

Ask the children if any of them know the story *Gumdrop has a Birthday*. If they do, invite them to share their knowledge with the class.

Tell the children that, in this lesson, they will focus on one extract from the story. Then they will answer

questions about it. Remind them that sometimes the answers to the questions will be clearly written in the extract, but that sometimes they may need to think a little harder and use their own ideas, supported by the extract.

Ask the children to read the extract individually or in pairs. Ask them to note down any words they do not understand. Discuss any unknown or unusual vocabulary before setting the children to work answering the questions in the Pupil Book. Try to avoid discussing the content of the extract until after the children have answered the questions.

Pupil practice

Pupil Book pages 4–6

Get started

The children copy the sentences and complete them using information from the text.

Answers

1. It was Gumdrop's <u>birthday</u>. [1 mark]

2. <u>Mr Oldcastle</u> invited several friends to celebrate. [1 mark]

3. The guests wished Gumdrop Many Happy <u>Returns</u>. [1 mark]

4. "For he's a jolly <u>good</u> fellow," they sang, [1 mark]

5. Horace sat on the ground and he looked very <u>fat</u>. [1 mark]

Try these

Assist the children if they ask for help with vocabulary, first discussing what they think the words might mean. Ask them to write sentences to answer the questions, explaining their answers with reference to the extract or their own experiences.

Suggested answers

1. *Before the guests sang to Gumdrop, they wished him Many Happy Returns.* *[example]*
2. Mr Oldcastle felt happy when the guests were singing. [1 mark]
3. He felt happy because his friends had come to celebrate with him. [1 mark]

4. The cake had been eaten by Horace. [1 mark]
5. I do not think Mr Oldcastle wanted this to happen because he was surprised that the cake was gone. [1 mark]

Now try these
Open-ended questions

1. Sentences should be from Mr Oldcastle's point of view, reacting to Horace eating Gumdrop's birthday cake. [3 marks max]
2. Answers should refer to presents that are car-related and some description of Mr Oldcastle's feelings about them. [3 marks max]
3. Pictures should be relevant to the extract, including details it mentions. [3 marks max]

Support, embed & challenge

Support

Use Unit 1 Resource 1: Ordering events to support the children in thinking about the structure of the story extract. Show them the template and discuss which part of the story might suit each section. Read the sentence starters and discuss with the children how they might finish each one before asking them to complete Unit 1 Resource 1: Ordering events.

Embed

Use Unit 1 Resource 2: A thank-you letter to encourage the children to think about what Mr Oldcastle might write in a thank-you letter to his guests. Read through the sentence starters and ask them to suggest what they might write. Remind them to imagine they are Mr Oldcastle, and to consider his feelings during the different events at the party. Encourage them to extend the letter by using their own ideas if they wish.

Challenge

Challenge the children to think about what they would do differently next time, if they were Mr Oldcastle. Ask them to plan next year's party for Gumdrop by making notes about what they would need, what they do – and how they would prevent another cake disaster!

Homework / Additional activities

Your birthday

Ask the children to make notes or write paragraphs about how they celebrate their own birthdays. Ask: 'Do you have a party?' 'Do you have a special family meal?' 'What is your favourite type of celebration?'

Collins Connect: Unit 1

Ask the children to complete Unit 1 (see Teach → Year 3 → Comprehension → Unit 1).

Unit 2: Poetry: 'Caterpillars'

Overview

English curriculum objectives

- Listen to and discuss a wide range of fiction, poetry, plays, non-fiction and reference books or textbooks
- Read books that are structured in different ways and reading for a range of purposes
- Use dictionaries to check the meanings of words they have read
- Identify themes and conventions in a wide range of books
- Prepare poems and play scripts to read aloud and to perform, showing understanding through intonation, tone, volume and action
- Discuss words and phrases that capture the reader's interest and imagination
- Recognise some different forms of poetry
- Check that the text makes sense to them, discussing their understanding and explaining the meaning of words in context
- Ask questions to improve their understanding of a text

- Draw inferences such as inferring characters' feelings, thoughts and motives from their actions, and justifying inferences with evidence
- Identify how language, structure and presentation contribute to meaning
- Participate in discussion about both books that are read to them and those they can read for themselves, taking turns and listening to what others say

Treasure House resources

- Comprehension Skills Pupil Book 3, Unit 2, pages 7–8
- Collins Connect Treasure House Comprehension Year 3, Unit 2
- Photocopiable Unit 2, Resource 1: Similes, page 67
- Photocopiable Unit 2, Resource 2: My caterpillars poem, page 68

Additional resources

- Dictionaries or the internet (optional)
- Other poems about caterpillars (optional)

Introduction

Teaching overview

'Caterpillars' is a descriptive poem about a familiar creature. It describes its subject in a positive way and is effective at both portraying caterpillars and engaging the reader. The description is simple, rhythmic (four beats per line) and uses rhyming couplets.

Introduce the poem

Ask the children to talk in pairs, taking turns to describe a caterpillar. Ask them to talk about how caterpillars look and behave. Then ask each pair to share their ideas with the class.

Tell the children that, in this lesson, they will focus on a poem that describes caterpillars. Then they will answer questions about it. Remind them that sometimes the answers to the questions will be clearly written in the poem, but that sometimes they may need to think a little harder and use their own ideas, supported by the text.

Ask the children to read the poem individually or in pairs. Ask them to note down any words they do not understand. Discuss any unknown or unusual vocabulary before setting the children to work answering the questions in the Pupil Book. Try to avoid discussing the content of the poem until after the children have answered the questions.

Pupil practice

Pupil Book pages 7–8

Get started

The children copy the sentences and complete them using information from the text.

Answers

1. Some have patches like <u>polka dots</u>   [1 mark]

2. Clinging to twigs with <u>tiny</u> feet   [1 mark]

3. But mostly green like the leaves they <u>chew</u>.   [1 mark]

4. Wiggling, woggling <u>up and down</u>   [1 mark]

5. <u>Always</u> looking for something to eat.   [1 mark]

Try these

Assist the children if they ask for help with vocabulary, first discussing what they think the words might mean. Ask them to write sentences to answer the questions, explaining their answers with reference to the text or their own experiences.

Suggested answers

1. *According to the poem, not all caterpillars are green. They can also be brown, yellow or blue.*　　　　　　　　　　*[example]*

2. Bristles are short, stiff hairs.　　　　[1 mark]

3. No, the caterpillars are not really painted.　[1 mark]

4. The poet says the caterpillars are painted to describe how bright they are and to compare them with clowns (which really are painted).　[1 mark]

5. 'Woggling' could be a cross between 'wiggling' and 'wobbling'.　　　　　　　[1 mark]

Now try these
Open-ended questions

1. The children should note down at least three reasonable ideas for similes.　[1 mark per simile]

2. Rhyming words: 'down'/'clown'; 'feet'/'eat'; 'spots'/'dots'; 'blue'/'chew'.　[1 mark]

　The children should write two pairs of rhyming lines about the caterpillars.　[4 marks]

3. Pictures should be relevant to the poem, including details it mentions.　[3 marks]

Support, embed & challenge

Support

Use Unit 2 Resource 1: Similes to support the children in understanding the concept of a simile. Remind them of the line in the poem, 'Painted as bright as a circus clown', and point out that the caterpillars are compared to circus clowns. Explain that we call a comparison like this a simile. Show the children the resource sheet and read the first part of each simile aloud. Then read some of the possible words that could complete the simile and talk about which might constitute a suitable ending. Ask the children, possibly in pairs, to draw lines to complete the similes appropriately. (**Answers** as slow as a snail; as cold as ice; as busy as a bee; as blind as a bat; as light as a feather; as bright as the sun; as sweet as sugar; as playful as a kitten; as flat as a pancake; as hard as iron)

Embed

Use Unit 2 Resource 2: My caterpillars poem to encourage the children to apply their learning by writing their own extension to the 'Caterpillars' poem in the same style. Ask the children to continue the poem by writing more about the caterpillars. Suggest they use four pairs of rhyming lines, as Eric Slater's poem does. Remind them of the line in the poem, 'Painted as bright as a circus clown', and point out that the caterpillars are compared to circus clowns. Explain that we call a comparison like this a simile. Ask them to try to use one new simile in their new lines.

Challenge

Challenge the children to think about a different creature and the qualities it has. Ask them to write notes and/or a poem about the creature in the same style as 'Caterpillars'.

Homework / Additional activities

More about caterpillars

Ask children to research and find out five interesting facts about caterpillars that they can share with the class.

Collins Connect: Unit 2

Ask the children to complete Unit 2 (see Teach → Year 3 → Comprehension → Unit 2).

Unit 3: Poetry: 'The Cow'

Overview

English curriculum objectives

- Listen to and discuss a wide range of fiction, poetry, plays, non-fiction and reference books or textbooks
- Read books that are structured in different ways and reading for a range of purposes
- Use dictionaries to check the meanings of words they have read
- Identify themes and conventions in a wide range of books
- Prepare poems and play scripts to read aloud and to perform, showing understanding through intonation, tone, volume and action
- Discuss words and phrases that capture the reader's interest and imagination
- Recognise some different forms of poetry
- Check that the text makes sense to them, discussing their understanding and explaining the meaning of words in context
- Ask questions to improve their understanding of a text

- Draw inferences such as inferring characters' feelings, thoughts and motives from their actions, and justifying inferences with evidence
- Identify how language, structure and presentation contribute to meaning
- Participate in discussion about both books that are read to them and those they can read for themselves, taking turns and listening to what others say

Treasure House resources

- Comprehension Skills Pupil Book 3, Unit 3, pages 9–10
- Collins Connect Treasure House Comprehension Year 3, Unit 3
- Photocopiable Unit 3, Resource 1: Comparing animals, page 69
- Photocopiable Unit 3, Resource 2: My animal poem, page 70

Additional resources

- Dictionaries or the internet (optional)
- Other poems about cows or pets (optional)

Introduction

Teaching overview

'The Cow' is a descriptive poem about a familiar creature. Like 'Caterpillars' in Unit 2, it describes its subject in a positive way and is effective at both portraying the animal and engaging the reader. The description is simple, rhythmic (four and then three beats per pair of lines) and rhyming (ABAB CDCD EFEF). It can be used to make a comparison with 'Caterpillars' in Unit 2.

Introduce the poem

Ask the children to tell you everything they know about cows. On the board, write 'The Cow' and create a mind map as the children contribute their ideas. Ask: 'What do cows look like?' 'How do they

behave?' 'What do they eat?' 'Where do they live?' Tell the children that, in this lesson, they will focus on a poem about a cow that is loved as a pet. Then they will answer questions about it. Remind them that sometimes they will find the answers to the questions written clearly in the poem, but that sometimes they may need to think a little harder and use their own ideas, supported by the poem.

Ask the children to read the poem individually or in pairs. Ask them to note down any words they do not understand. Discuss any unknown or unusual vocabulary before setting the children to work answering the questions in the Pupil Book. Try to avoid discussing the content of the poem until after the children have answered the questions.

Pupil practice

Pupil Book pages 9–10

Get started

The children copy the sentences and complete them using information from the poem.

Answers

1. She wanders <u>lowing</u> here and there.   [1 mark]
2. And blown by all the <u>winds that pass</u>   [1 mark]
3. And yet she <u>cannot</u> stray,   [1 mark]
4. I <u>love</u> with all my heart: [1 mark]
5. The <u>pleasant</u> light of day: [1 mark]

Try these

Assist the children if they ask for help with vocabulary, first discussing what they think the words might mean. Ask them to write sentences to answer the questions, explaining their answers with reference to the poem or their own experiences.

Suggested answers

1. *This poem is about a cow.*   *[example]*
2. The poet loves the cow because she gives him cream.   [1 mark]
3. The word 'lowing' means mooing.   [1 mark]
4. 'With all her might' means she tried her best.   [1 mark]
5. The cow doesn't go inside a shed.   [1 mark]

Now try these

Open-ended questions

1. Answers could refer to the 'pleasant open air' and 'pleasant light of day', or to the fact that the cow stands outside in the wind and rain, and 'cannot stray'.   [3 marks max]
2. Lines should be from the cow's point of view and refer to details from the poem.   [4 marks max]
3. Pictures should be relevant to the extract, including details it mentions.   [3 marks max]

Support, embed & challenge

Support

Use Unit 3 Resource 1: Comparing animals to support the children in extracting information from the poem and thinking about the qualities of the cow that it describes. Ask the children to fill in information about the cow from the poem and their own experiences. Discuss why the author may have chosen to include the information that they did in the poem. Then ask the children to choose two further animals and complete the chart.

Embed

Challenge the children to locate and write down the rhyming words in 'The Cow'. Ask them to work in pairs to find more words that rhyme with the

ones they have found. You could add a competitive element by challenging the children to see which pair can find most words.

Challenge

Use Unit 3 Resource 2: My animal poem to encourage the children to create their own poems using a style similar to that of 'The Cow'. Reread the poem, then read the structure and support provided on Unit 3 Resource 2. Ask the children to choose an animal and then begin to create their poems.

Homework / Additional activities

A pleasant poem

Ask children to write a short original poem inspired by the lines 'All in the pleasant open air,/The pleasant light of day:'. The poems could be in any style, and use any rhyme scheme and rhythm they like, including blank verse.

Collins Connect: Unit 3

Ask the children to complete Unit 3 (see Teach → Year 3 → Comprehension → Unit 3).

Unit 4: Non-fiction (news report): 'Monkey Business'

Overview

English curriculum objectives:

- Listen to and discuss a wide range of fiction, poetry, plays, non-fiction and reference books or textbooks
- Read books that are structured in different ways and reading for a range of purposes
- Use dictionaries to check the meanings of words they have read
- Identify themes and conventions in a wide range of books
- Discuss words and phrases that capture the reader's interest and imagination
- Check that the text makes sense to them, discussing their understanding and explaining the meaning of words in context
- Ask questions to improve their understanding of a text
- Draw inferences such as inferring characters' feelings, thoughts and motives from their actions, and justifying inferences with evidence
- Predict what might happen from details stated and implied

- Identify main ideas drawn from more than one paragraph and summarise these
- Identify how language, structure and presentation contribute to meaning
- Retrieve and record information from non-fiction
- Participate in discussion about both books that are read to them and those they can read for themselves, taking turns and listening to what others say

Treasure House resources

- Comprehension Skills Pupil Book 3, Unit 4, pages 11–13
- Collins Connect Treasure House Comprehension Year 3, Unit 4
- Photocopiable Unit 4, Resource 1: Find the facts, page 71
- Photocopiable Unit 4, Resource 2: A new news report, page 72

Additional resources

- Dictionaries or the internet (optional)
- Other local news reports (optional)

Introduction

Teaching overview

'Cheeky chimps on the motorway' is an amusing news report about monkeys that escape from a broken-down lorry transporting them to the zoo. The report provides a simple example of a formal, impersonal news report with characteristics such as eyewitness quotes and facts detailing what happened, when, where, why and to whom.

Introduce the news report

Ask the children if they ever read reports in newspapers. If they do, invite them to share their experiences with the class. Ask: 'Why do you think people read newspapers?' Clarify that newspapers provide us with both serious news information and

also entertaining reports of things that happen locally, nationally and internationally.

Tell the children that, in this lesson, they will focus on a newspaper report about some cheeky chimps. Then they will answer questions about it. Remind them that sometimes they will find the answers to the written clearly in the report, but that sometimes they may need to think a little harder and use their own ideas, supported by the text.

Ask the children to read the report individually or in pairs. Ask them to note down any words they do not understand. Discuss any unknown or unusual vocabulary before setting the children to work answering the questions in the Pupil Book. Try to avoid discussing the content of the report until after the children have answered the questions.

Pupil practice

Pupil Book pages 11–13

Get started

The children copy the sentences and complete them using information from the text.

Answers

1. Drivers were <u>surprised</u> to see monkeys running all over the road yesterday. [1 mark]
2. The lorry taking them to their new home at <u>Burwell</u> Zoo had broken down. [1 mark]

3. One of the monkeys <u>managed</u> to lift the latch on the door. [1 mark]

4. The monkeys looked like they were having <u>great</u> fun. [1 mark]

5. One even sat on top of the <u>police</u> car! [1 mark]

Try these

Assist the children if they ask for help with vocabulary, first discussing what they think the words might mean. Ask them to write sentences to answer the questions, explaining their answers with reference to the text or their own experiences.

Suggested answers

1. *The lorry had been going to Burwell Zoo. [example]*

2. In the end, the monkeys were caught and put back in the zoo. [1 mark]

3. Some drivers were angry but most were amused. [1 mark]

4. I don't think Inspector Baker was angry as he said the monkeys were having 'great fun' and called them 'cheeky chimps'. [2 marks]

5. I think he felt bad about making so much trouble. / I think he saw the funny side as not many people were angry. [2 marks]

Now try these

Open-ended questions

1. Answers should include an effort to understand how potential readers may feel. For example: *People may want to read it as they were affected by the traffic jam. / People may want to read it because it is an exciting story.* [3 marks max]

2. Sentences should be from a driver's point of view, reacting to the monkey's escape. The driver could be irate or amused. [3 marks max]

3. Pictures should be relevant to the news report and the children's previous answers about the feelings of the lorry driver and Inspector Baker. [3 marks max]

Support, embed & challenge

Support

Use Unit 4 Resource 1: Find the facts to support the children in extracting the facts from the newspaper report. Read through the chart and discuss where each piece of information is in the report. Discuss *why* the monkeys escaped in more detail: this information is not given in the text and will require inference.

Embed

Use Unit 4 Resource 2: A new news report to encourage the children to apply their learning by writing their own newspaper report about an incident involving animals. Read through the instructions and reminders at the top of the sheet, and support the children to make plans if necessary.

Challenge

Challenge the children to write a newspaper report about an event that has recently happened at school. Ask different pairs of children to write about different events or school-related topics, and then collate all of the articles to make a class newspaper.

Homework / Additional activities

Your birthday

Ask the children to find an interesting news report at home to bring in and show to the class. Ask them to isolate the facts detailing what happened, when, where, why and to whom.

Collins Connect: Unit 4

Ask the children to complete Unit 4 (see Teach → Year 3 → Comprehension → Unit 4).

Unit 5: Fiction (traditional story): 'Thunder and Lightning'

Overview

English curriculum objectives

- Listen to and discuss a wide range of fiction, poetry, plays, non-fiction and reference books or textbooks
- Read books that are structured in different ways and reading for a range of purposes
- Use dictionaries to check the meanings of words they have read
- Increase their familiarity with a wide range of books, including fairy stories, myths and legends, and retell some of these orally
- Identify themes and conventions in a wide range of books
- Discuss words and phrases that capture the reader's interest and imagination
- Check that the text makes sense to them, discussing their understanding and explaining the meaning of words in context
- Ask questions to improve their understanding of a text
- Draw inferences such as inferring characters' feelings, thoughts and motives from their actions, and justifying inferences with evidence

- Predict what might happen from details stated and implied
- Identify main ideas drawn from more than one paragraph and summarise these
- Identify how language, structure and presentation contribute to meaning
- Participate in discussion about both books that are read to them and those they can read for themselves, taking turns and listening to what others say

Treasure House resources

- Comprehension Skills Pupil Book 3, Unit 5, pages 14–16
- Collins Connect Treasure House Comprehension Year 3, Unit 5
- Photocopiable Unit 5, Resource 1: Retell the tale, page 73
- Photocopiable Unit 5, Resource 2: The tale of Rain, page 74

Additional resources

- Dictionaries or the internet (optional)
- Other traditional folk tales explaining natural phenomena (optional)

Introduction

Teaching overview

'Thunder and Lightning' provides a folk explanation of the natural phenomena that occur during storms: Thunder and Lightning are two badly behaved sheep banished to the sky. The text constitutes a good example of a traditional story or folk tale that provides a playful and personified explanation for phenomena that were (at the time) inexplicable.

Introduce the story

Ask the children if they know how people used to explain phenomena that they did not understand in the past. Elicit and confirm that people would commonly develop folk tales to try and explain things they did not understand. Give the example of the extreme weather of thunder and lightning.

Tell the children that, in this lesson, they will focus on a traditional story or folk tale from Nigeria in Africa that gives an explanation for what causes thunder and lightning. Then they will answer questions about it. Remind them that sometimes they will find the answers to the questions written clearly in the story, but that sometimes they may need to think a little harder and use their own ideas, supported by the text.

Ask the children to read the story individually or in pairs. Ask them to note down any words they do not understand. Discuss any unknown or unusual vocabulary before setting the children to work answering the questions in the Pupil Book. Try to avoid discussing the content of the story until after the children have answered the questions.

Pupil practice

Pupil Book pages 14–16

Get started

The children copy the sentences and complete them using information from the text.

Answers

1. <u>Thunder</u> and <u>Lightning</u> were two grumpy old sheep. [1 mark]
2. Thunder had an extremely <u>loud</u> voice. [1 mark]

3. The villagers complained about the <u>damage</u> and the <u>noise</u>. [1 mark]
4. The village chief sent the sheep to live in the <u>sky</u>. [1 mark]
5. Thunder still keeps the <u>villagers</u> awake at night. [1 mark]

Try these

Assist the children if they ask for help with vocabulary, first discussing what they think the words might mean. Ask them to write sentences to answer the questions, explaining their answers with reference to the folk tale or their own experiences.

Suggested answers

1. *Lightning lost his temper, knocked down trees and burnt crops.* *[example]*
2. In real life, lightning is a flash of electric fire from the sky during a storm. It can destroy things and causes fires. [2 marks]

3. They felt angry and fed up. [1 mark]
4. I think they wanted the village chief to stop the damage and the noise. [1 mark]
5. I don't think they were happy as the damage and noise continued even though the sheep were gone. [1 mark]

Now try these

Open-ended questions

1. Sentences should be from a villager's point of view, reacting to the continuing noise and damage coming from the sky. [3 marks max]
2. Retellings should attempt to consider the village chief's perspective, intentions and feelings. [3 marks max]
3. Pictures should be relevant to the story, including details it mentions. [3 marks max]

Support, embed & challenge

Support

Use Unit 5 Resource 1: Retell the tale to support the children in remembering what happened in the story. Read the sentence starters and discuss with children how they might finish each one before asking them to complete the resource sheet. They may also wish to add pictures.

Embed

Use Unit 5 Resource 2: The tale of Rain to encourage the children to apply their learning by writing their own tale or story about a naughty elephant called

Rain. Discuss how an elephant might be able to cause rain before asking the children to fill in the planning grid.

Challenge

Challenge the children to write a list of natural phenomena that they think people might not have been able to understand long ago (such as extreme weather, animals' individual characteristics and natural disasters). Discuss what folk tales they may have invented to explain these phenomena. Then ask the children to plan and begin writing their own versions of one of these folk tales.

Homework / Additional activities

Another explanation

Ask the children to research and read another example of a folk tale that explains a natural phenomenon. They should then present the tale to the class.

Collins Connect: Unit 5

Ask the children to complete Unit 5 (see Teach → Year 3 → Comprehension → Unit 5).

Unit 6: Fiction (fable): 'The Lion and the Mouse'

Overview

English curriculum objectives

- Listen to and discuss a wide range of fiction, poetry, plays, non-fiction and reference books or textbooks
- Read books that are structured in different ways and reading for a range of purposes
- Use dictionaries to check the meanings of words they have read
- Increase their familiarity with a wide range of books, including fairy stories, myths and legends, and retell some of these orally
- Identify themes and conventions in a wide range of books
- Discuss words and phrases that capture the reader's interest and imagination
- Check that the text makes sense to them, discussing their understanding and explaining the meaning of words in context
- Ask questions to improve their understanding of a text
- Draw inferences such as inferring characters' feelings, thoughts and motives from their actions, and justifying inferences with evidence

- Predict what might happen from details stated and implied
- Identify main ideas drawn from more than one paragraph and summarise these
- Identify how language, structure and presentation contribute to meaning
- Participate in discussion about both books that are read to them and those they can read for themselves, taking turns and listening to what others say

Treasure House resources

- Comprehension Skills Pupil Book 3, Unit 6, pages 17–19
- Collins Connect Treasure House Comprehension Year 3, Unit 6
- Photocopiable Unit 6, Resource 1: Making decisions, page 75
- Photocopiable Unit 6, Resource 2: Another moral tale, page 76

Additional resources

- Dictionaries or the internet (optional)
- Other fables by Aesop (optional)

Introduction

Teaching overview

'The Lion and the Mouse' is a version of the traditional fable by Aesop. It tells the tale of a lion that catches a mouse but takes pity on him and lets him go; later, the mouse returns the favour and saves the lion from a hunter. The moral of the tale could be read as 'the strong should not dismiss the weak' or 'don't belittle little things'.

Introduce the story

Ask the children if any of them know the fable of the lion and the mouse. If they do, invite them to share their knowledge with the class.

Tell the children that, in this lesson, they will focus on one version of the story, which was originally attributed to a storyteller called Aesop over 2,500 years ago. Then they will answer questions about it. Remind them that sometimes they will find the answers to the questions written clearly in the fable, but that sometimes they may need to think a little harder and use their own ideas, supported by the story.

Ask the children to read the story individually or in pairs. Ask them to note down any words they do not understand. Discuss any unknown or unusual vocabulary before setting the children to work answering the questions in the Pupil Book. Try to avoid discussing the content of the fable until after the children have answered the questions.

Pupil practice

Pupil Book pages 17–19

Get started

The children copy the sentences and complete them using information from the text.

Answers

1. A mouse happened to run over the paws of a sleeping lion. [1 mark]
2. He was about to crush the little animal. [1 mark]
3. "Please, mighty king of all the animals, spare me." [1 mark]

4. The idea that this tiny creature could ever help him <u>amused</u> the lion.   [1 mark]

5. The mouse ran to the <u>trap</u> and began to gnaw the ropes that bound the lion.   [1 mark]

Try these

Assist the children if they ask for help with vocabulary, first discussing what they think the words might mean. Ask them to write sentences to answer the questions, explaining their answers with reference to the text or their own experiences.

Suggested answers

1. *The characters in the story are a lion and a mouse.*   *[example]*

2. The mouse saved the lion by gnawing through the ropes of the hunter's net.   [1 mark]

3. You never know how important little things can be. / You should be kind to others as you never know when you may need their friendship. (Answers should not use the phrasing of the moral given in the story: 'Don't belittle little things.')   [1 mark]

4. The mouse saved the lion because the mouse was kind. / The mouse saved the lion to repay him for letting him go.   [1 mark]

5. I do not think the lion expected this to happen because he laughed when the mouse offered to help him.   [1 mark]

Now try these

Open-ended questions

1. Sentences should be from the lion's point of view, reacting to the mouse having saved him.   [3 marks max]

2. The six or more lines of dialogue should be appropriate to the events and the animals' feelings about them.   [3 marks max]

3. Pictures should be relevant to the fable, including details it mentions.   [3 marks max]

Support, embed & challenge

Support

Ask the children to think about how other children could be encouraged to be kinder to others. Ask them to create a poster or presentation to persuade others of the importance of kindness.

Embed

Use Unit 6 Resource 1: Making decisions to help the children to think about the choices the lion and the mouse faced when helping one another, and how things might have turned out differently if they had made different decisions. Ask them to complete the table, giving support through discussion where necessary.

Challenge

Use Unit 6 Resource 2: Another moral tale to encourage the children to apply their learning and develop their own stories with the same moral. They may use the example suggestion given, of a shark and a squid, to illustrate the tale's moral, but they do not have to.

Homework / Additional activities

Animal opposites

Ask the children to prepare lists of pairs of animals, such as the lion and the mouse or a shark and a squid, where one animal represents a bigger, stronger, fiercer creature and the other represents a smaller, more fragile creature. You could choose to add a competitive element by challenging the children to see who can write the longest list.

Collins Connect: Unit 6

Ask the children to complete Unit 6 (see Teach → Year 3 → Comprehension → Unit 6).

Unit 7: Fiction: 'The Dragon's Cold'

Overview

English curriculum objectives

- Listen to and discuss a wide range of fiction, poetry, plays, non-fiction and reference books or textbooks
- Read books that are structured in different ways and reading for a range of purposes
- Use dictionaries to check the meanings of words they have read
- Increase their familiarity with a wide range of books, including fairy stories, myths and legends, and retell some of these orally
- Identify themes and conventions in a wide range of books
- Discuss words and phrases that capture the reader's interest and imagination
- Check that the text makes sense to them, discussing their understanding and explaining the meaning of words in context
- Ask questions to improve their understanding of a text
- Draw inferences such as inferring characters' feelings, thoughts and motives from their actions, and justifying inferences with evidence

- Predict what might happen from details stated and implied
- Identify main ideas drawn from more than one paragraph and summarise these
- Identify how language, structure and presentation contribute to meaning
- Participate in discussion about both books that are read to them and those they can read for themselves, taking turns and listening to what others say

Treasure House resources

- Comprehension Skills Pupil Book 3, Unit 7, pages 20–22
- Collins Connect Treasure House Comprehension Year 3, Unit 7
- Photocopiable Unit 7, Resource 1: Before and after, page 77
- Photocopiable Unit 7, Resource 2: How Duncan caught a cold, page 78

Additional resources

- Dictionaries or the internet (optional)
- *The Dragon's Cold* by John Talbot, whole text (optional)

Introduction

Teaching overview

The Dragon's Cold is a story about a dragon who has been rejected by his friends and family because he has a cold that has put out his fire. The dragon is found by some children who set about helping him.

Introduce the extract

Ask the children if any of them know the story *The Dragon's Cold*. If they do, invite them to share their knowledge with the class. Then ask them what they know about dragons from other stories and again ask them to share their experiences.

Tell the children that, in this lesson, they will focus on one extract from the story. Then they will answer questions about it. Remind them that sometimes they will find the answers to the questions written clearly in the extract, but that sometimes they may need to think a little harder and use their own ideas, supported by the text.

Ask the children to read the extract individually or in pairs. Ask them to note down any words they do not understand. Discuss any unknown or unusual vocabulary before setting the children to work answering the questions in the Pupil Book. Try to avoid discussing the content of the extract until after the children have answered the questions.

Pupil practice   Pupil Book pages 20–22

Get started

The children copy the sentences and complete them using information from the text.

Answers

1. "Look at this," said <u>Mimi</u>.   [1 mark]

2. "Let's get <u>out</u> of here!"   [1 mark]

3. "Oh, don't go," said the dragon.
"I won't <u>hurt</u> you."   [1 mark]

4. "It's <u>completely</u> put my fire out." [1 mark]

5. "We'll think of <u>something</u>." [1 mark]

Try these

Assist the children if they ask for help with vocabulary, first discussing what they think the words might mean. Ask them to write sentences to answer the questions, explaining their answers with reference to the text or their own experiences.

Suggested answers

1. *The characters in this story are Mimi, Alex, Roland, Spike and the dragon.* [example]

2. Duncan is the dragon. [1 mark]

3. Duncan feels sad because he has a cold. It has put out his fire so his friends and family have sent him away. [2 marks]

4. When the children first find the dragon, they feel scared. I know this because they all shout, "Let's get out of here!" [1 mark]

5. At the end of the extract, the children are no longer scared. I know this because Mimi offers to take care of the dragon and Alex agrees with her. [1 mark]

Now try these

Open-ended questions

1. Sentences should be from Duncan's point of view, reacting to Mimi's offer to take care of him and the children's kindness. [3 marks max]

2. Descriptions should be relatively powerful, and include details of how the dragon looks, smells and sounds, how the child would feel and what they would say. [3 marks max]

3. Pictures should be relevant to the extract and the previous answer, including details it mentions. [3 marks max]

Support, embed & challenge

Support

Ask the children to think about how having a cold makes them feel. Ask them to write a list or some descriptive sentences to explain how a cold affects them.

Embed

Use Unit 7 Resource 1: Before and after to support the children in thinking more deeply about how Duncan's cold affected him. Encourage them to use the extract, their own knowledge of having a cold and their imagination to complete the sections in the chart.

Challenge

Use Unit 7 Resource 2: How Duncan caught a cold to encourage the children to think about what may have happened in the story before the events described in the extract. Talk through the sections on the template, referring to the extract and drawing on the children's imaginations to build up the story.

Homework / Additional activities

What happens next?

Ask the children to think about what could happen next in the story. They could show their ideas through pictures and/or writing, perhaps creating comic strips or storyboards to explain their plans.

Collins Connect: Unit 7

Ask the children to complete Unit 7 (see Teach → Year 3 → Comprehension → Unit 7).

Review unit 1: Fiction: 'The Selfish Giant'

Pupil Book pages 23–24

Get started

The children copy the sentences and complete them using information from the text.

Answers

1. Every day after school, the <u>children</u> crept into the Giant's garden. [1 mark]

2. But then, no one had told them they <u>couldn't</u>. [1 mark]

3. They climbed the <u>trees</u> and hid in the bushes. [1 mark]

4. They played <u>football</u> and ran races over the lawns. [1 mark]

5. He'd been travelling for a long time and was feeling <u>tired</u> and cross. [1 mark]

Try these

Assist the children if they ask for help with vocabulary, first discussing what they think the words might mean. Ask them to write sentences to answer the questions, explaining their answers with reference to the extract or their own experiences.

Suggested answers

1. *The children crept into the Giant's garden every day after school.* *[example]*

2. The activities the children did in the Giant's garden were: climbing trees, hiding in bushes, playing football, running races, lying in the grass and listening to the birds singing. [6 marks]

3. The children didn't know what the Giant looked like because he had been away for years and years. [1 mark]

4. It isn't clear if the children were allowed to play in the garden: no one had told them they could, but no one had told them they couldn't. [1 mark]

5. I think the Giant will be angry because he is tired and cross / because it is his private garden. / I don't think the Giant will mind, as he hasn't been using his garden. [1 mark]

Now try these

Open-ended questions

1. Sentences should be from the children's point of view, reacting to the Giant coming home. [3 marks max]

2. Sentences should describe the Giant (including how he looks, smells and sounds), describe how a child might react to him and suggest an appropriate way of greeting or questioning him. [3 marks max]

3. Pictures should be relevant to the extract, including details it mentions. [3 marks max]

Unit 8: Non-fiction (letter): 'Gran's New House'

Overview

English curriculum objectives

- Listen to and discuss a wide range of fiction, poetry, plays, non-fiction and reference books or textbooks
- Read books that are structured in different ways and reading for a range of purposes
- Use dictionaries to check the meanings of words they have read
- Identify themes and conventions in a wide range of books
- Discuss words and phrases that capture the reader's interest and imagination
- Check that the text makes sense to them, discussing their understanding and explaining the meaning of words in context
- Ask questions to improve their understanding of a text
- Draw inferences such as inferring characters' feelings, thoughts and motives from their actions, and justifying inferences with evidence
- Predict what might happen from details stated and implied

- Identify main ideas drawn from more than one paragraph and summarise these
- Identify how language, structure and presentation contribute to meaning
- Retrieve and record information from non-fiction
- Participate in discussion about both books that are read to them and those they can read for themselves, taking turns and listening to what others say

Treasure House resources

- Comprehension Skills Pupil Book 3, Unit 8, pages 25–27
- Collins Connect Treasure House Comprehension Year 3, Unit 8
- Photocopiable Unit 8, Resource 1: Asking questions, page 79
- Photocopiable Unit 8, Resource 2: A letter home, page 80

Additional resources

- Dictionaries or the internet (optional)
- Other examples of letters, real or fictional (optional)

Introduction

Teaching overview

'Gran's New House' provides an example of a typical (fictional) recount letter. Gran writes to her grandchildren to tell them about her new house. The letter contains characteristics common to informal letter writing, and provides opportunity for discussion about recounting events, using the past tense and organising information into paragraphs.

Introduce the text

Ask the children if they have ever moved house, or if they know anyone else who has moved house. If they do, invite them to share their knowledge with the class. Then talk briefly about the different reasons people move house and again ask them to share their experiences.

Tell the children that, in this lesson, they will focus on a letter about moving house. Then they will answer questions about it. Remind them that sometimes they will find the answers to the questions written clearly in the letter, but that sometimes they may need to think a little harder and use their own ideas, supported by the text.

Ask the children to read the letter individually or in pairs. Ask them to note down any words they do not understand. Discuss any unknown or unusual vocabulary before setting the children to work answering the questions in the Pupil Book. Try to avoid discussing the content of the letter until after the children have answered the questions.

Pupil practice

Pupil Book pages 25–27

Get started

The children copy the sentences and complete them using information from the text.

Answers

1. We moved into our new house just <u>three</u> days ago. [1 mark]

2. From our <u>front</u> windows we can see the sea. [1 mark]

3. At the back we have lovely <u>views</u> of the hills. [1 mark]

4. The journey should have only taken about <u>two</u> hours! [1 mark]

5. I thought you may like to come and <u>stay</u> for a few days. [1 mark]

Try these

Assist the children if they ask for help with vocabulary, first discussing what they think the words might mean. Ask them to write sentences to answer the questions, explaining their answers with reference to the letter or their own experiences.

Suggested answers

1. *The letter was written to Annie, Tim and Jenny.* *[example]*

2. The best things about the new house are the views of the sea and the hills. [1 mark]

3. Gran thinks it feels strange not living in the same town as the children any more. [1 mark]

4. Grandad lives with Gran. [1 mark]

5. I think Gran is glad they moved, as she says, "I think we are going to like it." / I think Gran is not glad they moved, as I think she misses the children. [1 mark]

Now try these

Open-ended questions

1. Sentences should be from Annie's, Tim's or Jenny's point of view, reacting to Gran's move away. [3 marks max]

2. Diary entries should be from Annie's, Tim's or Jenny's point of view. They should include detailed descriptions of the child's feelings about the move and discussion of whether or not they want to visit Gran. [3 marks max]

3. Pictures should be relevant to the letter, including details it mentions. [3 marks max]

Support, embed & challenge

Support

Use Unit 8 Resource 1: Asking questions to help the children isolate the information given, and not given, in the letter. Once they have reread the letter, ask them what questions they could ask Gran. Talk about the importance of being interested in other people's lives and asking questions as a way of maintaining a family relationship. Show how the questions can be categorised as those about the moving process and those about the new house. Ask the children to list as many questions as they can.

Embed

Use Unit 8 Resource 2: A letter home to encourage the children to imagine they are one of the children in the letter and on a visit to Gran in the holidays. Ask them to use the template to write a letter home to Mum and Dad, telling them about the new house and about the visit.

Challenge

Challenge the children to write a diary entry as though they were Gran, and to write honestly about her reasons for moving house and her worries about not seeing her grandchildren.

Homework / Additional activities

My new house

Ask the children to write letters to relatives or family friends, describing their own houses as though they have just moved in. Ask them to consider the best and less good parts of the move.

Collins Connect: Unit 8

Ask the children to complete Unit 8 (see Teach → Year 3 → Comprehension → Unit 8).

Unit 9: Non-fiction (information text): 'Ants'

Overview

English curriculum objectives

- Listen to and discuss a wide range of fiction, poetry, plays, non-fiction and reference books or textbooks
- Read books that are structured in different ways and reading for a range of purposes
- Use dictionaries to check the meanings of words they have read
- Identify themes and conventions in a wide range of books
- Discuss words and phrases that capture the reader's interest and imagination
- Check that the text makes sense to them, discussing their understanding and explaining the meaning of words in context
- Ask questions to improve their understanding of a text
- Draw inferences such as inferring characters' feelings, thoughts and motives from their actions, and justifying inferences with evidence
- Predict what might happen from details stated and implied

- Identify main ideas drawn from more than one paragraph and summarise these
- Identify how language, structure and presentation contribute to meaning
- Retrieve and record information from non-fiction
- Participate in discussion about both books that are read to them and those they can read for themselves, taking turns and listening to what others say

Treasure House resources

- Comprehension Skills Pupil Book 3, Unit 9, pages 28–30
- Collins Connect Treasure House Comprehension Year 3, Unit 9
- Photocopiable Unit 9, Resource 1: Quick quiz, page 81
- Photocopiable Unit 9, Resource 2: Insect fact file, page 82

Additional resources

- Dictionaries or the internet (optional)
- Other information texts on insects (optional)

Introduction

Teaching overview

'Ants' is a non-fiction information text. It presents factual information about where ants live, different types of ants and the jobs ants do. The children are able to explore how language, structure and presentation in a non-fiction text contribute to meaning, as the text features subheadings, short paragraphs and photographs.

Introduce the information text

Ask the children what they know about ants and invite them to share their knowledge with the class.

Tell the children that, in this lesson, they will focus on one extract from an information book about ants. Then they will answer questions about it. Remind them that sometimes they will find the answers to the questions written clearly in the extract, but that sometimes they may need to think a little harder and use their own ideas, supported by the text.

Ask the children to read the extract individually or in pairs. Ask them to note down any words they do not understand. Discuss any unknown or unusual vocabulary before setting the children to work answering the questions in the Pupil Book. Try to avoid discussing the content of the text until after the children have answered the questions.

Pupil practice

Pupil Book pages 28–30

Get started

The children copy the sentences and complete them using information from the text.

Answers

1. Tiny <u>tunnels</u> lead into the nest. [1 mark]

2. Each nest is a mass of tunnels and <u>rooms</u>. [1 mark]
3. In every nest there are <u>three</u> types of ant. [1 mark]
4. Queen ants have <u>wings</u>. [1 mark]
5. The <u>small ants</u> are the worker ants. [1 mark]

Try these

Assist the children if they ask for help with vocabulary, first discussing what they think the words might mean. Ask them to write sentences to answer the questions, explaining their answers with reference to the text or their own experiences.

Suggested answers

1. *The queen ant lives in one room.* *[example]*
2. The worker ants do the most different kinds of jobs. [1 mark]
3. No, big male ants do not collect food. Worker ants collect food. [2 marks]
4. Queen ants and big male ants have wings. [1 mark]
5. The worker ants dig all the rooms. [1 mark]

Now try these

Open-ended questions

1. Look for three clear facts written in the child's own words. These could be taken from the extract or may be from the child's own knowledge. [3 marks max]
2. Pictures should be accurate in details such as the queen ant's size and wings. Labels should be accurate and clear. [3 marks max]
3. Pictures should be accurate in details such as a network of tunnels and rooms, with a queen ant in her room, winged big male ants with her and worker ants gathering food, feeding young ants, digging or protecting the nest. Labels should be accurate and clear. [3 marks max]

Support, embed & challenge

Support

Use Unit 9 Resource 1: Quick quiz to support the children in checking how well they have understood the text. The children could work independently or in supported groups to discuss and answer each question.

Embed

Use Unit 9 Resource 2: Insect fact file to encourage the children to apply their learning by planning their own fact files on insects of their choice, then ask them to use their plans to write their fact files. You may wish to provide time in the library or on the internet for them to research facts about their chosen insects.

Challenge

Challenge the children to think further about the difference between a fact and an opinion. Ask them to look at their definitions in the dictionary. Then ask them to discuss and write some opinions about ants. You could then ask them to create a poster showing the difference.

Homework / Additional activities

Favourite facts

Ask the children to collect a list of facts about a topic that interests them. It could be an animal, a book or a hobby. You could specify a number of facts to collect, or leave it as an open-ended challenge. Ask the children to be prepared to share their facts with a group or the class.

Collins Connect: Unit 9

Ask the children to complete Unit 9 (see Teach → Year 3 → Comprehension → Unit 9).

Unit 10: Non-fiction (information text): 'On Holiday'

Overview

English curriculum objectives

- Listen to and discuss a wide range of fiction, poetry, plays, non-fiction and reference books or textbooks
- Read books that are structured in different ways and reading for a range of purposes
- Use dictionaries to check the meanings of words they have read
- Identify themes and conventions in a wide range of books
- Discuss words and phrases that capture the reader's interest and imagination
- Check that the text makes sense to them, discussing their understanding and explaining the meaning of words in context
- Ask questions to improve their understanding of a text
- Draw inferences such as inferring characters' feelings, thoughts and motives from their actions, and justifying inferences with evidence
- Predict what might happen from details stated and implied
- Identify main ideas drawn from more than one paragraph and summarise these
- Identify how language, structure and presentation contribute to meaning
- Retrieve and record information from non-fiction
- Participate in discussion about both books that are read to them and those they can read for themselves, taking turns and listening to what others say

Treasure House resources

- Comprehension Skills Pupil Book 3, Unit 10, pages 31–33
- Collins Connect Treasure House Comprehension Year 3, Unit 10
- Photocopiable Unit 10, Resource 1: A letter of complaint, page 83
- Photocopiable Unit 10, Resource 2: Information pack, page 84

Additional resources

- Dictionaries or the internet (optional)
- Other holiday information packs, such as welcome packs from caravan parks, to be used for comparison (optional)

Introduction

Teaching overview

'Sandy Bay Holiday Park' is a leaflet for a (fictional) holiday park that gives instructions in the form of 'do' and 'don't' rules for visitors staying at the park. The children are able to explore how language, structure and presentation in a non-fiction text contribute to meaning, as the text features lists with introductory paragraphs.

Introduce the text

Ask the children if they have ever been on holiday to a holiday park. If they have, ask what information or leaflets their family was given when they arrived. Allow the children to share their experiences, but keep the focus of the conversation on the information they were given to read.

Tell the children that, in this lesson, they will focus on a welcome leaflet for a holiday park, giving visitors some rules to follow. Then they will answer questions about it. Remind them that sometimes they will find the answers to the questions written clearly in the text, but that sometimes they may need to think a little harder and use their own ideas, supported by the text.

Ask the children to read the instructions individually or in pairs. Ask them to note down any words they do not understand. Discuss any unknown or unusual vocabulary before setting the children to work answering the questions in the Pupil Book. Try to avoid discussing the content of the instructions until after the children have answered the questions.

Pupil practice

Pupil Book pages 31–33

Get started

The children copy the sentences and complete them using information from the text.

Answers

1. Welcome to <u>Sandy Bay</u> Holiday Park. [1 mark]
2. May we offer some <u>advice</u>. [1 mark]
3. <u>Walk</u> around the park to get your bearings. [1 mark]
4. Visit our supermarket to <u>stock up</u> with provisions. [1 mark]
5. Enjoy a relaxed holiday, away from the <u>hurly-burly</u> of everyday life! [1 mark]

Try these

Assist the children if they ask for help with vocabulary, first discussing what they think the words might mean. Ask them to write sentences to answer the questions, explaining their answers with reference to the text or their own experiences.

Suggested answers

1. *You can get more information at the information centre.* [example]

2. There are three pieces of advice on the leaflet. There are five rules. [2 marks]
3. The park has rules to ensure that guests have a relaxed holiday. [1 mark]
4. The word 'provisions' means supplies of food and drink. The word 'unaccompanied' means not with anyone else. I think 'hurly-burly' means noisiness and being busy. [3 marks]
5. Open-ended question: Accept any well-reasoned choices. [1 mark]

Now try these

Open-ended questions

1. Questions should be from a visitor's point of view, and not be answered by the text. [3 marks max]
2. Accept any well-structured numbered list that provides information relevant for the holiday park and not included in the leaflet. [3 marks max]
3. The new layout of the leaflet should be useful and it should present the information clearly. [3 marks max]

Support, embed & challenge

Support

Use Unit 10 Resource 1: A letter of complaint to support the children in thinking closely about the content of the text. Ask them to imagine that they are guests at the holiday park. They are annoyed! Ask each child to choose whether he or she is annoyed with the rules because they think they are too restrictive, or annoyed with other guests breaking the rules. Ask the children to write a letter of complaint to the holiday park, making sure they refer to the leaflet in their letter.

Embed

Challenge the children to think about why rules matter. Ask them to read the rules on the leaflet again and to justify each one, using information from the leaflet and their imagination.

Challenge

Use Unit 10 Resource 2: Information pack to encourage the children to apply their learning by designing their own holiday park information packs. Ask the children to read through the sections on the planning template and discuss their ideas with a partner before writing them down.

Homework / Additional activities

Real-life leaflets

Discuss where the children might find examples of information leaflets: in supermarkets, local tourist information offices, theatres, council offices or museums. Ask the children to find and bring in a couple of examples of leaflets, and to be prepared to discuss them with a group or the class.

Collins Connect: Unit 10

Ask the children to complete Unit 10 (see Teach → Year 3 → Comprehension → Unit 10).

Unit 11: Non-fiction (poster): 'Fun on Bikes'

Overview

English curriculum objectives

- Listen to and discuss a wide range of fiction, poetry, plays, non-fiction and reference books or textbooks
- Read books that are structured in different ways and reading for a range of purposes
- Use dictionaries to check the meanings of words they have read
- Identify themes and conventions in a wide range of books
- Discuss words and phrases that capture the reader's interest and imagination
- Check that the text makes sense to them, discussing their understanding and explaining the meaning of words in context
- Ask questions to improve their understanding of a text
- Draw inferences such as inferring characters' feelings, thoughts and motives from their actions, and justifying inferences with evidence
- Predict what might happen from details stated and implied

- Identify main ideas drawn from more than one paragraph and summarise these
- Identify how language, structure and presentation contribute to meaning
- Retrieve and record information from non-fiction
- Participate in discussion about both books that are read to them and those they can read for themselves, taking turns and listening to what others say

Treasure House resources

- Comprehension Skills Pupil Book 3, Unit 11, pages 34–36
- Collins Connect Treasure House Comprehension Year 3, Unit 11
- Photocopiable Unit 11, Resource 1: The bike competition, page 85
- Photocopiable Unit 11, Resource 2: New event poster, page 86

Additional resources

- Dictionaries or the internet (optional)
- Other examples of posters advertising events (optional)

Introduction

Teaching overview

'Fun on Bikes' provides a poster advertising an event (which is fictional): The Annual Young Bikers' Championship. It includes a bold headline and image to catch the reader's attention, and provides a good opportunity for locating specific information necessary for the promotion of any event, such as its time, location and the available facilities.

Introduce the text

Ask the children what the purpose of posters is. Collect ideas and clarify that posters can be an effective way of sharing information, such as the promotion of events including competitions or shows.

Tell the children that, in this lesson, they will focus on a poster that advertises an event. Then they will answer questions about it. Remind them that sometimes they will find the answers to the questions written clearly on the poster, but that sometimes they may need to think a little harder and use their own ideas, supported by the text.

Ask the children to read the text individually or in pairs. Ask them to note down any words they do not understand. Discuss any unknown or unusual vocabulary before setting the children to work answering the questions in the Pupil Book. Try to avoid discussing the content of the poster until after the children have answered the questions.

Pupil practice

Pupil Book pages 34–36

Get started

The children copy the sentences and complete them using information from the text.

Answers

1. This poster advertises the Annual Young Bikers' Championship. [1 mark]

2. The competition is on Saturday 25th October. [1 mark]
3. If you are a rider, you can get in for free. [1 mark]
4. Spectators need to pay £1. [1 mark]

5. You must be seven/7 years old or older to take part. [1 mark]

Try these

Assist the children if they ask for help with vocabulary, first discussing what they think the words might mean. Ask them to write sentences to answer the questions, explaining their answers with reference to the text or their own experiences.

Suggested answers

1. *Seniors compete from 12.30 to 3.00.* [example]

2. The competition is being held at Crossfield Farm, Westergate. [1 mark]

3. The competition happens annually / every year. [1 mark]

4. Yes, you can get something to eat or drink as there is a refreshment tent. [1 mark]

5. I think under-7 bikers aren't allowed to enter in case the race is too fast / the track is too dangerous for them. [1 mark]

Now try these

Open-ended questions

1. This poster is telling people about a bike-riding competition called The Young Bikers' Championship. It is advertising the competition to encourage people to take part, and to come and watch it. [3 marks max]

2. This is a good poster because it is clear and easy to read. It has a bold heading and a colourful picture that helps to catch the reader's attention. It helps the reader because it contains all the information someone may need to enjoy the competition, such as its time, place and cost. [3 marks max]

3. Diary entries should be from a spectator's point of view. Look for references to the details given on the poster. [3 marks max]

Support, embed & challenge

Support

Use Unit 11 Resource 1: The bike competition to support the children in relating details they have read in the poster to a real-life/narrative context. Ask groups to read the story extract (or read it to them) and discuss the ways the information in the story matches the information given on the poster. Ask: 'Can you work out how old Jenny is?'

Embed

Use Unit 11 Resource 2: New event poster to encourage children to apply their learning about posters by planning their own event posters. After the children have used the planning grid, you could ask them to create their posters. Ask: 'How will your poster grab people's attention?'

Challenge

Ask the children to recall the leaflet studied in Unit 10. Challenge them to think about which is the best way to give people information: a poster or a leaflet. Ask groups to discuss and make notes on the pros and cons of both forms, and then to reach a conclusion of which may be better (for certain types of event) and why.

Homework / Additional activities

Powerful posters

Ask children to find real-life examples of event posters, and to bring in posters or pictures of them to share and discuss with the class. Ask them to consider what features have been used on the posters, and how effective they are.

Collins Connect: Unit 11

Ask the children to complete Unit 11 (see Teach → Year 3 → Comprehension → Unit 11).

Unit 12: Poetry: 'Roger the Dog'

Overview

English curriculum objectives

- Listen to and discuss a wide range of fiction, poetry, plays, non-fiction and reference books or textbooks
- Read books that are structured in different ways and reading for a range of purposes
- Use dictionaries to check the meanings of words they have read
- Identify themes and conventions in a wide range of books
- Prepare poems and play scripts to read aloud and to perform, showing understanding through intonation, tone, volume and action
- Discuss words and phrases that capture the reader's interest and imagination
- Recognise some different forms of poetry
- Check that the text makes sense to them, discussing their understanding and explaining the meaning of words in context
- Ask questions to improve their understanding of a text

- Draw inferences such as inferring characters' feelings, thoughts and motives from their actions, and justifying inferences with evidence
- Identify how language, structure and presentation contribute to meaning
- Participate in discussion about both books that are read to them and those they can read for themselves, taking turns and listening to what others say

Treasure House resources

- Comprehension Skills Pupil Book 3, Unit 12, pages 37–39
- Collins Connect Treasure House Comprehension Year 3, Unit 12
- Photocopiable Unit 12, Resource 1: Rhyming words, page 87
- Photocopiable Unit 12, Resource 2: A new pet poem, page 88

Additional resources

- Dictionaries or the internet (optional)
- Other poems about pets (optional)

Introduction

Teaching overview

'Roger the Dog' is an example of a poem that uses rhyming couplets to create a humorous tone and engaging pattern. It is written in the first person and describes the amusing but frustrating behaviour of the speaker's lazy pet dog.

Introduce the poem

Ask the children if they have a pet dog, or know someone who does. If they do, invite them to share their knowledge of its behaviour with the class.

Tell the children that, in this lesson, they will focus on a poem that describes the behaviour of a pet dog.

Then they will answer questions about it. Remind them that sometimes they will find the answers to the questions written clearly in the poem, but that sometimes they may need to think a little harder and use their own ideas, supported by the text.

Ask the children to read the poem individually or in pairs. Ask them to note down any words they do not understand. Discuss any unknown or unusual vocabulary before setting the children to work answering the questions in the Pupil Book. Try to avoid discussing the content of the poem until after the children have answered the questions.

Pupil practice

Pupil Book pages 37–39

Get started

The children copy the sentences and complete them using information from the text.

Answers

1. Asleep he <u>wheezes</u> at his ease.   [1 mark]

2. He bakes his head as if he were a <u>loaf</u> of bread.   [1 mark]
3. You <u>lug</u> him like a log.   [1 mark]
4. He <u>will not</u> romp.   [1 mark]
5. He digs down deep, <u>like a miner</u>, into sleep.   [1 mark]

Try these

Assist the children if they ask for help with vocabulary, first discussing what they think the words might mean. Ask them to write sentences to answer the questions, explaining their answers with reference to the text or their own experiences.

Suggested answers

1. *When Roger lies by the fire, he makes sure his head is warm.* [example]

2. Roger eats his dinner quickly and greedily. This explains the words 'gobble and chomp'. [2 marks]

3. No, Roger does not like to run around. I know this because the poem says 'He will not race, he will not romp'. [1 mark]

4. Roger's two favourite things to do are eating and sleeping. [1 mark]

5. The poet says Roger is 'like a log' because he is heavy, doesn't move on his own and has to be dragged or rolled. [3 marks]

Now try these

Open-ended questions

1. The children should note down at least three reasonable ideas for similes. [1 mark per simile]

2. Rhyming words: 'ease'/'fleas'; 'head'/'bread'; 'dog'/'log'; 'foot'/'put'; 'exercise'/'eyes'; 'romp'/'chomp'; 'wish'/'dish'; 'deep'/'sleep'. [1 mark]

   Open-ended question: The children should write two pairs of rhyming lines about Roger. [4 marks max]

3. Pictures should feature a dog eating or sleeping, and be relevant to the poem, including details it mentions. [3 marks max]

Support, embed & challenge

Support

Use Unit 12 Resource 1: Rhyming words to support the children in thinking further about the rhyming couplets used in the poem. Ask them to use the resource sheet to help them to find the words in the poem that rhyme with the words in the bubbles before adding more rhyming words to each list.

Embed

Encourage the children to apply their understanding of the poem's content by writing an extended diary entry as though they are Roger's owner. Their writing should not be in rhyme, but should include good and accurate descriptions of Roger's behaviour.

Challenge

Use Unit 12 Resource 2: A new pet poem to challenge the children to write their own funny pet poems, first using the planning grid to record their ideas.

Homework / Additional activities

Pet poems

Ask the children to research and write out or print another poem about a pet, humorous if possible, to share with the class.

Collins Connect: Unit 12

Ask the children to complete Unit 12 (see Teach → Year 3 → Comprehension → Unit 12).

Unit 13: Fiction (classic): 'The Tale of Peter Rabbit'

Overview

English curriculum objectives

- Listen to and discuss a wide range of fiction, poetry, plays, non-fiction and reference books or textbooks
- Read books that are structured in different ways and reading for a range of purposes
- Use dictionaries to check the meanings of words they have read
- Increase their familiarity with a wide range of books, including fairy stories, myths and legends, and retell some of these orally
- Identify themes and conventions in a wide range of books
- Discuss words and phrases that capture the reader's interest and imagination
- Check that the text makes sense to them, discussing their understanding and explaining the meaning of words in context
- Ask questions to improve their understanding of a text
- Draw inferences such as inferring characters' feelings, thoughts and motives from their actions, and justifying inferences with evidence
- Predict what might happen from details stated and implied
- Identify main ideas drawn from more than one paragraph and summarise these
- Identify how language, structure and presentation contribute to meaning
- Participate in discussion about both books that are read to them and those they can read for themselves, taking turns and listening to what others say

Treasure House resources

- Comprehension Skills Pupil Book 3, Unit 13, pages 40–42
- Collins Connect Treasure House Comprehension Year 3, Unit 13
- Photocopiable Unit 13, Resource 1: What was Peter thinking? page 89
- Photocopiable Unit 13, Resource 2: Peter in trouble, page 90

Additional resources

- Dictionaries or the internet (optional)
- *The Tale of Peter Rabbit* by Beatrix Potter, whole text (optional)

Introduction

Teaching overview

The Tale of Peter Rabbit tells the classic story of a naughty rabbit called Peter, who finds himself trapped and pursued in Mr. McGregor's garden. A picture of the setting is built up through the descriptions of Peter's actions, what he sees and where he hides.

Introduce the extract

Ask the children if any of them know the story *The Tale of Peter Rabbit*. If they do, invite them to share their knowledge with the class.

Tell the children that, in this lesson, they will focus on one extract from the story. Then they will answer

questions about it. Remind them that sometimes they will find the answers to the questions written clearly in the extract, but that sometimes they may need to think a little harder and use their own ideas, supported by the text.

Ask the children to read the extract individually or in pairs. Ask them to note down any words they do not understand. Discuss any unknown or unusual vocabulary before setting the children to work answering the questions in the Pupil Book. Try to avoid discussing the content of the extract until after the children have answered the questions.

Pupil practice

Pupil Book pages 40–42

Get started

The children copy the sentences and complete them using information from the text.

Answers

1. Peter lived under the roots of a <u>big fir tree</u>. [1 mark]

2. He was <u>always a problem</u> for his mother.   [1 mark]

3. "You may go into the fields or down the lane, but don't go into <u>Mr. McGregor's</u> garden." [1 mark]

4. Feeling rather <u>sick</u>, he went to look for some parsley. [1 mark]

5. Mr. McGregor was <u>on his hands and knees</u> planting out cabbages. [1 mark]

Try these

Assist the children if they ask for help with vocabulary, first discussing what they think the words might mean. Ask them to write sentences to answer the questions, explaining their answers with reference to the text or their own experiences.

Suggested answers

1. *Peter was allowed to go into the fields or down the lane.* [example]

2. Peter was not allowed to go into Mr. McGregor's garden. [1 mark]

3. Old Mrs. Rabbit is afraid her children will be put into a pie if they go into Mr. McGregor's garden because that's what happened to their father. [2 marks]

4. I think Peter went into Mr. McGregor's garden anyway because he is very naughty / because he is not afraid of Mr. McGregor / because he wanted to eat Mr. McGregor's vegetables. [1 mark]

5. I think Peter is afraid of Mr. McGregor now, and is sorry that he went into the garden. / I think Peter believes he will escape and is glad that he went into the garden. [1 mark]

Now try these
Open-ended questions

1. Sentences should be from old Mrs. Rabbit's point of view, reacting to Peter going into Mr. McGregor's garden and acknowledging the fact that Peter's father was put into a pie by Mrs. McGregor. [3 marks max]

2. Retellings should attempt to consider Mr. McGregor's perspective, intentions and feelings. [3 marks max]

3. Pictures should be relevant to the extract, including details it mentions. [3 marks max]

Support, embed & challenge

Support

Use Unit 13 Resource 1: What was Peter thinking? to support the children in exploring what Peter might have felt and thought at each point through the story. Ask them to consider why Peter was naughty and disobeyed his mother.

Embed

Challenge the children to think about what daily life would be like for Peter and his family. Ask them to discuss and then write a schedule for a typical day in the life of a rabbit. Encourage them to think chronologically through the day, from the time the rabbits wake up to the time they go to bed.

Challenge

The extract says that Peter 'was always a problem for his mother, causing trouble and getting into scrapes'. Use Unit 13 Resource 2: Peter in trouble to encourage the children to write their own tales about an earlier time that Peter caused trouble.

Homework / Additional activities

Other books by Beatrix Potter

Ask children to research and find out the titles of some of Beatrix Potter's other stories. Ask them to bring in a book by Beatrix Potter from home, if they have one.

Collins Connect: Unit 13

Ask the children to complete Unit 13 (see Teach → Year 3 → Comprehension → Unit 13).

Unit 14: Fiction (classic): 'The Owl Who Was Afraid of the Dark'

Overview

English curriculum objectives

- Listen to and discuss a wide range of fiction, poetry, plays, non-fiction and reference books or textbooks
- Read books that are structured in different ways and reading for a range of purposes
- Use dictionaries to check the meanings of words they have read
- Increase their familiarity with a wide range of books, including fairy stories, myths and legends, and retell some of these orally
- Identify themes and conventions in a wide range of books
- Discuss words and phrases that capture the reader's interest and imagination
- Check that the text makes sense to them, discussing their understanding and explaining the meaning of words in context
- Ask questions to improve their understanding of a text
- Draw inferences such as inferring characters' feelings, thoughts and motives from their actions, and justifying inferences with evidence

- Predict what might happen from details stated and implied
- Identify main ideas drawn from more than one paragraph and summarise these
- Identify how language, structure and presentation contribute to meaning
- Participate in discussion about both books that are read to them and those they can read for themselves, taking turns and listening to what others say

Treasure House resources

- Comprehension Skills Pupil Book 3, Unit 14, pages 43–45
- Collins Connect Treasure House Comprehension Year 3, Unit 14
- Photocopiable Unit 14, Resource 1: A 'proper' owl, page 91
- Photocopiable Unit 14, Resource 2: What happens next? page 92

Additional resources

- Dictionaries or the internet (optional)
- *The Owl Who Was Afraid of the Dark* by Jill Tomlinson, whole text (optional)

Introduction

Teaching overview

The Owl Who Was Afraid of the Dark is a humorous story about a young owl named Plop, who is afraid of the dark. His parents become increasingly fed up with his fear, and they encourage him to speak to people and other animals to learn about the dark.

Introduce the extract

Ask the children if any of them know the story *The Owl Who Was Afraid of the Dark*. If they do, invite them to share their knowledge with the class. Then ask what they know about real owls and, again, ask them to share their experiences.

Tell the children that, in this lesson, they will focus on one extract from the story. Then they will answer questions about it. Remind them that sometimes they will find the answers to the questions written clearly in the extract, but that sometimes they may need to think a little harder and use their own ideas, supported by the text.

Ask the children to read the extract individually or in pairs. Ask them to note down any words they do not understand. Discuss any unknown or unusual vocabulary before setting the children to work answering the questions in the Pupil Book. Try to avoid discussing the content of the extract until after the children have answered the questions.

Pupil practice

Pupil Book pages 43–45

Get started

The children copy the sentences and complete them using information from the text.

Answers

1. Mother Owl was getting <u>fed up</u> with Plop. [1 mark]
2. "Little girls don't have <u>tails</u>." [1 mark]
3. His <u>landing</u> was a little better than usual. [1 mark]
4. "Actually, I'm a <u>Barn Owl</u>." [1 mark]
5. "I've never met an <u>owl</u> before." [1 mark]

Try these

Assist the children if they ask for help with vocabulary, first discussing what they think the words might mean. Ask them to write sentences to answer the questions, explaining their answers with reference to the text or their own experiences.

Suggested answers

1. *The little girl thought Plop was a fluffy ball.*

[example]

2. She thought this because Plop bounced when he hit the ground. [1 mark]

3. Plop thinks the girl has a tail because his mother said she had a ponytail, and he doesn't understand what ponytails are. [2 marks]

4. I think Plop is cross with the girl because she thought he was a ball, she said he wasn't a real owl, he doesn't understand about her ponytail and he doesn't really want to ask her about the dark. [3 marks]

5. I don't think the girl likes Plop as she thinks he is being huffy. / I think the girl does like Plop as he's fluffy and she's excited to meet an owl. [1 mark]

Now try these

Open-ended questions

1. Sentences should be from Mother Owl's point of view, reacting to Plop's conversation with the girl. [3 marks max]

2. The diary entry should be from the girl's point of view, and refer to the details about her meeting with Plop in the extract. [3 marks max]

3. Pictures should be relevant to the extract, including details it mentions and using speech bubbles appropriately. [3 marks max]

Support, embed & challenge

Support

Use Unit 14 Resource 1: A 'proper' owl to support children in exploring the ways in which the two main characters in the extract do not behave as they expect each other to. Ask them to fill in the chart to show the different expectations and realities.

Embed

Ask the children to think about why Plop might be scared of the dark. Ask them to write a letter to Plop, giving him advice and reassurance about the dark from their own points of view.

Challenge

Use Unit 14 Resource 2: What happens next? to encourage the children to plan their own continuation scenes. They could then begin to write their scenes in detail.

Homework / Additional activities

Amazing owls

Ask the children to research and find six interesting facts about owls that they can share with the class.

Collins Connect: Unit 14

Ask the children to complete Unit 14 (see Teach → Year 3 → Comprehension → Unit 14).

Review unit 2: Non-fiction (information text): 'Air-Sea Rescue'

Pupil Book pages 46–48

Get started

The children copy the sentences and complete them using information from the text.

Answers

1. Air-sea rescue crews use different kinds of aircraft and boats to help people who get into <u>trouble</u> at sea. [1 mark]

2. All these craft carry first-aid equipment such as stretchers, blankets and <u>oxygen</u> masks. [1 mark]

3. The <u>helicopter</u> is the most useful aircraft for air-sea rescue. [1 mark]

4. It can hover in the air above a <u>person</u> in the sea or above a boat. [1 mark]

5. A winchman is lowered down from a helicopter on a wire to <u>pluck</u> people from the water, or from the decks of boats. [1 mark]

Try these

Assist the children if they ask for help with vocabulary, first discussing what they think the words might mean. Ask them to write sentences to answer the questions, explaining their answers with reference to the text or their own experiences.

Suggested answers

1. *Air-sea rescue crews help people who get into trouble at sea.* *[example]*

2. Air-sea rescue crafts have first-aid equipment (such as stretchers, blankets and oxygen masks), navigation equipment, radar equipment and night-vision goggles on board. [4 marks max]

3. I think a winch operator uses the winch to lower the winchman down to the sea. [1 mark]

4. I think a rescue swimmer swims out to help people in trouble in the sea. [1 mark]

5. A boat might be more helpful than a helicopter if there are lots of people to be rescued / if there is very bad weather. [2 marks max]

Now try these

Open-ended questions

1. Sentences should be from the winchman's point of view, relating to the rescue he/she is about to perform. [3 marks max]

2. The three facts should be in the child's own words, and accurate according to the text. [3 marks max]

3. Pictures and labels should be accurate and clear, and relate to the information given in the text. They should include an appropriate vehicle or aircraft, rescue equipment, and crew members performing their duties. [3 marks max]

Unit 15: Non-fiction (information text): 'Funny Feeders'

Overview

English curriculum objectives

- Listen to and discuss a wide range of fiction, poetry, plays, non-fiction and reference books or textbooks
- Read books that are structured in different ways and reading for a range of purposes
- Use dictionaries to check the meanings of words they have read
- Identify themes and conventions in a wide range of books
- Discuss words and phrases that capture the reader's interest and imagination
- Check that the text makes sense to them, discussing their understanding and explaining the meaning of words in context
- Ask questions to improve their understanding of a text
- Draw inferences such as inferring characters' feelings, thoughts and motives from their actions, and justifying inferences with evidence
- Predict what might happen from details stated and implied

- Identify main ideas drawn from more than one paragraph and summarise these
- Identify how language, structure and presentation contribute to meaning
- Retrieve and record information from non-fiction
- Participate in discussion about both books that are read to them and those they can read for themselves, taking turns and listening to what others say

Treasure House resources

- Comprehension Skills Pupil Book 3, Unit 15, pages 49–51
- Collins Connect Treasure House Comprehension Year 3, Unit 15
- Photocopiable Unit 15, Resource 1: True or false? page 93
- Photocopiable Unit 15, Resource 2: Information leaflet, page 94

Additional resources

- Dictionaries or the internet (optional)
- Other information texts about exotic animals or plants (optional)

Introduction

Teaching overview

'Funny Feeders' is an example of an engaging information text that will appeal to children. It displays characteristics typically associated with non-fiction information texts, such as impersonal language, subheadings, photographs and key words in bold.

Introduce the text

Ask the children if they can remember some of the features that are typical in a non-fiction information text. Take suggestions and note down the features mentioned, such as headings, subheadings, photographs or diagrams, paragraphs and facts.

Tell the children that, in this lesson, they will focus on an extract from an information text about the funny eating habits of different animals and plants. Then they will answer questions about it. Remind them that sometimes they will find the answers to the questions written clearly in the text, but that sometimes they may need to think a little harder and use their own ideas, supported by the text.

Ask the children to read the text individually or in pairs. Ask them to note down any words they do not understand. Discuss any unknown or unusual vocabulary before setting the children to work answering the questions in the Pupil Book. Try to avoid discussing the content of the text until after the children have answered the questions.

Pupil practice

Pupil Book pages 49–51

Get started

The children copy the sentences and complete them using information from the text.

Answers

1. Many frogs have long <u>tongues</u>. [1 mark]

2. They can <u>shoot them out</u> extremely quickly. [1 mark]
3. Many insects eat <u>plants</u>. [1 mark]
4. Venus flytraps are plants that <u>attack insects</u>! [1 mark]
5. Mistletoe, which grows in the branches of a tree, is a <u>parasite</u>. [1 mark]

Try these

Assist the children if they ask for help with vocabulary, first discussing what they think the words might mean. Ask them to write sentences to answer the questions, explaining their answers with reference to the text or their own experiences.

Suggested answers

1. *Venus flytraps close their leaves to trap flies, which they can then digest.* [example]

2. Mistletoe feeds on other plants. [1 mark]

3. Vultures do not kill other animals for food. They eat animals that are already dead. [1 mark]

4. Mosquitoes and fleas can feed off humans. [1 mark]

5. According to the text, some insects feed off other insects or blood instead of plants. [1 mark]

Now try these

Open-ended questions

1. Answers should recognise that the main point of the extract is that some plants and animals feed in unusual ways. [1 mark]

2. Look for three clear facts written in the child's own words. These could be taken from the text or may be from the child's own knowledge. [3 marks max]

3. Pictures and information boxes should be accurate in details such as the Venus flytrap closing its leaves and the fly becoming trapped. [3 marks max]

Support, embed & challenge

Support

Use Unit 15 Resource 1: True or false? to support the children in practising their reading memory skills. Ask them to try answering the questions without rereading the extract to find the answers. Then, when they have attempted the questions, they could use rereading to check their answers. (**Answers** False; True; True; False; False; True; True; False; True; False; True)

Embed

Use Unit 15 Resource 2: Information leaflet to encourage the children to use the information from the text to create their own information leaflets on the topic of 'funny feeders'. Enable them to conduct additional research in books or on the internet.

Challenge

Challenge the children to think about their own eating habits. Ask them to make notes and write a descriptive paragraph to explain, as though to an alien, the ways in which humans eat, what we eat and how we eat.

Homework / Additional activities

Parasite presentations

Ask the children to find out more about parasites. Ask them to compile a list of different parasites using internet research and/or library books, and to be prepared to present their findings.

Collins Connect: Unit 15

Ask the children to complete Unit 15 (see Teach → Year 3 → Comprehension → Unit 15).

Unit 16: Poetry: 'The Car Trip'

Overview

English curriculum objectives

- Listen to and discuss a wide range of fiction, poetry, plays, non-fiction and reference books or textbooks
- Read books that are structured in different ways and reading for a range of purposes
- Use dictionaries to check the meanings of words they have read
- Identify themes and conventions in a wide range of books
- Prepare poems and play scripts to read aloud and to perform, showing understanding through intonation, tone, volume and action
- Discuss words and phrases that capture the reader's interest and imagination
- Recognise some different forms of poetry
- Check that the text makes sense to them, discussing their understanding and explaining the meaning of words in context
- Ask questions to improve their understanding of a text

- Draw inferences such as inferring characters' feelings, thoughts and motives from their actions, and justifying inferences with evidence
- Identify how language, structure and presentation contribute to meaning
- Participate in discussion about both books that are read to them and those they can read for themselves, taking turns and listening to what others say

Treasure House resources

- Comprehension Skills Pupil Book 3, Unit 16, pages 52–54
- Photocopiable Unit 16, Resource 1: The car-trip story, page 95
- Photocopiable Unit 16, Resource 2: Mum's view, page 96

Additional resources

- Dictionaries or the internet (optional)
- 'The Car Trip' by Michael Rosen, whole poem (optional)

Introduction

Teaching overview

'The Car Trip' is a humorous narrative poem that tells the tale of two children on a car journey with their mother. It is a particularly good example of a poem that encourages children to draw inferences regarding characters' feelings, thoughts and motives from their actions, and to justify inferences with evidence.

Introduce the poem

Ask the children if they like going on long car journeys, and about what conversations typically take place in their cars. Invite them to share their experiences with the class.

Tell the children that, in this lesson, they will focus on part of a poem about two children on a car trip with their mother. Then they will answer questions about it. Remind them that sometimes they will find the answers to the questions written clearly in the poem, but that sometimes they may need to think a little harder and use their own ideas, supported by the text.

Ask the children to read the poem individually or in pairs. Ask them to note down any words they do not understand. Discuss any unknown or unusual vocabulary before setting the children to work answering the questions in the Pupil Book. Try to avoid discussing the content of the poem until after the children have answered the questions.

Pupil practice

Pupil Book pages 52–54

Get started

The children copy the sentences and complete them using information from the poem.

Answers

1. I want you two to be <u>good</u>. [1 mark]
2. I'm driving and I can't drive properly / if you two are going <u>mad</u> in the back. [1 mark]

3. You <u>never</u> tell him off. [1 mark]
4. Now he's <u>biting</u> his nails. [1 mark]
5. And Mum tries to be <u>exciting</u> again: [1 mark]

Try these

Assist the children if they ask for help with vocabulary, first discussing what they think the words might mean. Ask them to write sentences to answer the questions, explaining their answers with reference to the poem or their own experiences.

Suggested answers

1. *The children in the poem are going on a very long car journey.* *[example]*

2. Mum says she can't drive properly if the children are 'going mad in the back' of the car. [1 mark]

3. The children ask Mum: 'Can I have a drink?', 'Can I open my window?', 'Can I have a sweet?' and 'Are we nearly there?' [4 marks]

4. The capital letters show the phrase 'The Moaning' to have increased importance. It is a recognised and regular event so has adopted the form of a proper name. [3 marks max]

5. I think the children are moaning because they are bored / they do not get on / they do not like long car journeys. [2 marks max]

Now try these

Open-ended questions

1. Sentences should be from Mum's point of view, explaining why she tells them to look out of the window. She is trying to distract the children from moaning and arguing with one another by pointing out the lamp post and the tree. [3 marks max]

2. Verses should include four new things about which the children could moan on a car trip. For example: 'I'm hot', 'I'm cold', 'Can you turn the music up/down', 'I'm bored', 'There's a bug in the car', 'I'm squashed', 'I feel sick'. [3 marks max]

3. Pictures should be relevant to the poem, including details it mentions. [3 marks max]

Support, embed & challenge

Support

Use Unit 16 Resource 1: The car-trip story to support the children in looking at the poem more closely, by turning it into a story. Read through the structure provided on the template, and talk about what could be written in each section. Refer back to the poem to add in the things the children moaned about. Suggest that the children add any extra details that they would like to make it their own.

Embed

Use Unit 16 Resource 2: Mum's view to encourage the children to consider Mum's thoughts and feelings throughout the extract. The children should retell the extract as a telephone conversation between Mum and her friend, thinking about Mum's point of view throughout.

Challenge

Challenge the children to think about the way in which dialogue is used in the poem by creating a performance that recreates its events as the dialogue described. The children could also improvise a continuation of the scene, and note this down to create an extra verse.

Homework / Additional activities

On our journeys...

Ask the children to think about, and ask family members about, how they and any siblings behave on long journeys. Ask the children to write notes about the things they do and say on journeys, ready to share with the class. You could use this information to create a new class poem.

Unit 17: Playscript: 'The Gigantic Turnip Tug'

Overview

English curriculum objectives

- Listen to and discuss a wide range of fiction, poetry, plays, non-fiction and reference books or textbooks
- Read books that are structured in different ways and reading for a range of purposes
- Use dictionaries to check the meanings of words they have read
- Increase their familiarity with a wide range of books, including fairy stories, myths and legends, and retell some of these orally
- Identify themes and conventions in a wide range of books
- Prepare poems and play scripts to read aloud and to perform, showing understanding through intonation, tone, volume and action
- Discuss words and phrases that capture the reader's interest and imagination
- Check that the text makes sense to them, discussing their understanding and explaining the meaning of words in context
- Ask questions to improve their understanding of a text

- Draw inferences such as inferring characters' feelings, thoughts and motives from their actions, and justifying inferences with evidence
- Predict what might happen from details stated and implied
- Identify main ideas drawn from more than one paragraph and summarise these
- Identify how language, structure and presentation contribute to meaning
- Participate in discussion about both books that are read to them and those they can read for themselves, taking turns and listening to what others say

Treasure House resources

- Comprehension Skills Pupil Book 3, Unit 17, pages 55–57
- Photocopiable Unit 17, Resource 1: Finding the features, page 97
- Photocopiable Unit 17, Resource 2: Costumes and setting, page 98

Additional resources

- Dictionaries or the internet (optional)
- *The Gigantic Turnip Tug* by Lois Walker, whole text (optional)

Introduction

Teaching overview

The Gigantic Turnip Tug is a playscript version of the classic traditional tale of *The Enormous Turnip*. The extract here uses five speaking parts and lends itself to being performed in groups. It also features a memorable rhyming chorus that is suitable for the class to learn by heart and recite together. It includes typical playscript features, such as speaker names, colons and stage directions.

Introduce the extract

Ask the children if any of them know (any versions of) the story *The Enormous Turnip*. If they do, invite them to share their knowledge with the class.

Tell the children that, in this lesson, they will focus on an extract from a playscript version of the traditional tale. Then they will answer questions about it. Remind them that sometimes they will find the answers to the questions written clearly in the extract, but that sometimes they may need to think a little harder and use their own ideas, supported by the text.

Ask the children to read the extract individually or in pairs. Ask them to note down any words they do not understand. Discuss any unknown or unusual vocabulary before setting the children to work answering the questions in the Pupil Book. Try to avoid discussing the content of the extract until after the children have answered the questions.

Pupil practice

Pupil Book pages 55–57

Get started

Answers

1. Once upon a time, a little old <u>man</u> and a little old woman… [1 mark]
2. One <u>morning</u> they left the farmhouse and said… [1 mark]
3. *(They <u>mime</u> planting seeds.)* [1 mark]
4. Spring passed and the vegetables grew <u>big</u> and round. [1 mark]
5. They didn't eat this <u>turnip</u> because it was more than big and round. [1 mark]

Try these

Assist the children if they ask for help with vocabulary, first discussing what they think the words might mean. Ask them to write sentences to answer the questions, explaining their answers with reference to the text or their own experiences.

Suggested answers

1. *The little old man and the little old woman lived in a tiny farmhouse near an overgrown garden.* [example]

2. The little old man and the little old woman walk to the garden bed. [1 mark]

3. It was summer when the old man and woman ate the vegetables: the script says 'Spring passed'. [1 mark]

4. I think there are three narrators because it makes the play sound more interesting / it gives more people a chance to join in with the play. [2 marks max]

5. The sentences in *italics* are stage directions. / The sentences in *italics* tell the actors how to move. [2 marks max]

Now try these
Open-ended questions

1. Sentences should be from the old man or woman's point of view, giving reasons why they hadn't yet eaten the gigantic turnip. [3 marks max]

2. Continuations should use playscript features and layout, such as speakers' names followed by colons, no speech marks for dialogue, a new line for each new speaker and possibly stage directions. They should be consistent with and relevant to the content of the extract. [3 marks max]

3. Pictures should be relevant to the extract, including details it mentions. They should feature the little old man and woman planting seeds in a garden setting. [3 marks max]

Support, embed & challenge

Support

Use Unit 17 Resource 1: Finding the features to support the children in familiarising themselves with the features of a playscript. They should label the features with the terms supplied. They could also use coloured pens and highlighters to help them identify the features.

Embed

Ask the children to get into small groups to act out the playscript. Ask them to pay attention to who speaks when, and to all the stage directions. They could then improvise the next part of the story. (If they don't already know the story, ask them simply to use their imaginations.)

Challenge

Use Unit 17 Resource 2: Costumes and setting to challenge the children to think about how the play scene should look. They should note down costume ideas for each character, all the props needed and ideas about how the stage should look.

Homework / Additional activities

How vegetables grow

Ask the children to research and write two lists: one of vegetables that grow under the ground and one of vegetables that grow above the ground. Ask them if they were surprised by any of their findings. Add a competitive element by challenging the children to see who has listed the most types of vegetables.

Unit 18: Fiction (traditional tale): 'The House in the Forest'

Overview

English curriculum objectives

- Listen to and discuss a wide range of fiction, poetry, plays, non-fiction and reference books or textbooks
- Read books that are structured in different ways and reading for a range of purposes
- Use dictionaries to check the meanings of words they have read
- Increase their familiarity with a wide range of books, including fairy stories, myths and legends, and retell some of these orally
- Identify themes and conventions in a wide range of books
- Discuss words and phrases that capture the reader's interest and imagination
- Check that the text makes sense to them, discussing their understanding and explaining the meaning of words in context
- Ask questions to improve their understanding of a text
- Draw inferences such as inferring characters' feelings, thoughts and motives from their actions, and justifying inferences with evidence

- Predict what might happen from details stated and implied
- Identify main ideas drawn from more than one paragraph and summarise these
- Identify how language, structure and presentation contribute to meaning
- Participate in discussion about both books that are read to them and those they can read for themselves, taking turns and listening to what others say

Treasure House resources

- Comprehension Skills Pupil Book 3, Unit 18, pages 58–60
- Photocopiable Unit 18, Resource 1: Helga's character, page 99
- Photocopiable Unit 18, Resource 2: Two diaries, page 100

Additional resources

- Dictionaries or the internet (optional)
- *The House in the Forest* by Janet Foxley, whole text (optional)

Introduction

Teaching overview

The House in the Forest is a retelling of the classic traditional tale *Hansel and Gretel*. In the original, Hansel and Gretel are a brother and sister who are captured by a child-eating witch after being abandoned in the woods by their starving parents. In the version used for this unit, the story has a modern-day setting. The children are sent to the woods to collect firewood to sell after their father, a carpenter, has all his tools stolen. (In this version, the story concludes when the old woman who kidnaps the children is revealed to be the thief.)

Introduce the extract

Ask the children if any of them know (any versions of) the story *Hansel and Gretel*. If they do, invite them to share their knowledge with the class.

Tell the children that, in this lesson, they will focus on one extract from a modern retelling of the story. Then they will answer questions about it. Remind them that sometimes they will find the answers to the questions written clearly in the extract, but that sometimes they may need to think a little harder and use their own ideas, supported by the text.

Ask the children to read the extract individually or in pairs. Ask them to note down any words they do not understand. Discuss any unknown or unusual vocabulary before setting the children to work answering the questions in the Pupil Book. Try to avoid discussing the content of the extract until after the children have answered the questions.

Pupil practice

Pupil Book pages 58–60

Get started

The children copy the sentences and complete them using information from the text.

Answers

1. She looked longingly at the half loaf on the <u>breakfast</u> table.   [1 mark]
2. "It's time you were off to the <u>forest</u>."   [1 mark]

3. She quickly put the loaf in the cupboard, <u>locked</u> the door and slipped the key into her pocket. [1 mark]

4. "The forest is dark and full of <u>strange</u> noises." [1 mark]

5. And they were in enough <u>trouble</u> already. [1 mark]

Try these

Assist the children if they ask for help with vocabulary, first discussing what they think the words might mean. Ask them to write sentences to answer the questions, explaining their answers with reference to the extract or their own experiences.

Suggested answers

1. *Helga locked the bread in the cupboard. [example]*

2. Helga said that Hansel couldn't have another slice of bread because there would be nothing left for supper. [1 mark]

3. Gretel was looking longingly at the half loaf of bread on the breakfast table because she was still hungry and wanted some of the bread she could see. [1 mark]

4. The family makes money by selling the firewood the children collect. [1 mark]

5. Gretel feels afraid of the forest. I know this because she says it is dark and full of strange noises, and wants her father to go with them. [1 mark]

Now try these
Open-ended questions

1. Sentences should be from Hansel and Gretel's father's of view, and could reflect his sorrow over losing his first wife, his guilt at being unemployed, his desire to help his children and his obedience of his new wife. [3 marks max]

2. New versions should be from Helga's perspective, and reflect how her character and attitudes are detailed in the extract. They could mention her irritation at having to feed a family with no money, at the children's hunger and fear of the forest, and at her husband's inability to find a job. [3 marks max]

3. Pictures should be relevant to the extract, including details it mentions. They should feature the children walking into the forest. [3 marks max]

Support, embed & challenge

Support

Ask the children to think about what the ending of the story might be. Ask them to talk about possible endings in groups and then decide on an ending they can share with the class. Provide guidance by suggesting events that really occur in the story if required (see 'Teaching overview' above).

Embed

Use Unit 18 Resource 1: Helga's character to support the children in exploring the character of Helga, the children's stepmother. The children should reread the text to find information that they can use in the profile. If the information is not easily located in the extract, discuss with the children what the answers could be, encouraging them to use their imagination.

Challenge

Use Unit 18 Resource 2: Two diaries to encourage the children to think about the points of view of Hansel and Dad. Talk about how the same event or situation might be perceived differently by different characters. The children should write one paragraph from the point of view of Hansel and one from the point of view of Dad, describing the events of the day.

Homework / Additional activities

What happens next?

Ask the children to research and read a version of the whole story of *Hansel and Gretel*. If possible, source and provide the full text of *The House in the Forest*. Then discuss how the modern version has updated the story events.

Unit 19: Fiction (modern): 'Spider McDrew and the Egyptians'

Overview

English curriculum objectives

- Listen to and discuss a wide range of fiction, poetry, plays, non-fiction and reference books or textbooks
- Read books that are structured in different ways and reading for a range of purposes
- Use dictionaries to check the meanings of words they have read
- Increase their familiarity with a wide range of books, including fairy stories, myths and legends, and retell some of these orally
- Identify themes and conventions in a wide range of books
- Discuss words and phrases that capture the reader's interest and imagination
- Check that the text makes sense to them, discussing their understanding and explaining the meaning of words in context
- Ask questions to improve their understanding of a text
- Draw inferences such as inferring characters' feelings, thoughts and motives from their actions, and justifying inferences with evidence

- Predict what might happen from details stated and implied
- Identify main ideas drawn from more than one paragraph and summarise these
- Identify how language, structure and presentation contribute to meaning
- Participate in discussion about both books that are read to them and those they can read for themselves, taking turns and listening to what others say

Treasure House resources

- Comprehension Skills Pupil Book 3, Unit 19, pages 61–63
- Photocopiable Unit 19, Resource 1: Romans and Egyptians, page 101
- Photocopiable Unit 19, Resource 2: Spider's character, page 102

Additional resources

- Dictionaries or the internet (optional)
- *Spider McDrew and the Egyptians* by Alan Durrant, whole text (optional)

Introduction

Teaching overview

Spider McDrew and the Egyptians is a story about the adventures of a boy called Spider. He is described in an earlier part of the book as 'a hopeless case': he often gets things wrong, as he tends to think longer and harder about things than those around him do. In this story, Spider and his class visit a local museum to learn about life in Roman times. However, Spider becomes distracted and ends up in the wrong part of the museum.

Introduce the extract

Ask the children if any of them know the character of Spider McDrew. If they do, invite them to share their knowledge with the class. Reveal and discuss Spider's character (see above). Then ask the children

what they know about Romans and Egyptians. Again, ask them to share their experiences.

Tell the children that, in this lesson, they will focus on an extract from the story *Spider McDrew and the Egyptians*. Then they will answer questions about it. Remind them that sometimes they will find the answers to the questions written clearly in the extract, but that sometimes they may need to think a little harder and use their own ideas, supported by the text.

Ask the children to read the extract individually or in pairs. Ask them to note down any words they do not understand. Discuss any unknown or unusual vocabulary before setting the children to work answering the questions in the Pupil Book. Try to avoid discussing the content of the extract until after the children have answered the questions.

Pupil practice
Pupil Book pages 61–63

Get started

The children copy the sentences and complete them using information from the text.

Answers

1. Spider's class was <u>learning</u> about the Romans. [1 mark]

2. Soon they were going to dress up in Roman <u>costumes</u> and do a school assembly. [1 mark]

3. "Please sir, I went to see the <u>mummies</u>, sir," Darren Kelly said breathlessly. [1 mark]

4. "Mummies had their brains pulled out through their noses," Neil Phillips added <u>happily</u>. [1 mark]

5. Spider <u>smiled</u>. "I've got a mummy," he said. [1 mark]

Try these

Assist the children if they ask for help with vocabulary, first discussing what they think the words might mean. Ask them to write sentences to answer the questions, explaining their answers with reference to the text or their own experiences.

Suggested answers

1. *Spider's class was learning about the Romans.* *[example]*

2. The children were more interested in seeing the Egyptian mummies at the museum. [1 mark]

3. The class was going to the museum to prepare for their school assembly about the Romans. [1 mark]

4. The class laughed at Spider because he said 'I've got a mummy'. They thought he was confusing Egyptian mummies with mothers. [2 marks]

5. I think Spider felt embarrassed when the class laughed at him. / I think Spider felt frustrated because he didn't mean what they thought he meant. [1 mark]

Now try these

Open-ended questions

1. Sentences should be from Spider's point of view, explaining that he had meant to refer to a small Egyptian mummy model, not to his mother. [3 marks max]

2. Answers should refer to Mr Smithers's plan to show the children Roman exhibits at the museum, and the children's desire to see the Egyptian mummies instead. [3 marks max]

3. Pictures should be relevant to the extract, including details it mentions. [3 marks max]

Support, embed & challenge

Support

Use Unit 19 Resource 1: Romans and Egyptians to provide some background information about the Romans and the Egyptians. Ask the children to read through the information and to find the facts mentioned in the extract.

Embed

Use Unit 19 Resource 2: Spider's character to support the children in exploring the character of Spider McDrew. The children should reread the text carefully to extract information that they can use in the profile. If the information is not easily located in the extract, discuss with the children what they think Spider is like, encouraging them to infer ideas from the text and expand their own thoughts about Spider.

Challenge

Challenge the children to think about and plan the assembly Spider's class is going to do on their Romans topic. Ask: 'How would the assembly start?' 'What Roman things could the class present?' 'How would every child in the class get a turn to do something?' 'How would the assembly finish?' You might provide some research time and books to support the children's ideas.

Homework / Additional activities

Museum must-sees!

Ask the children to find out what exhibits are in their nearest museum. Ask them to choose which they would be most interested in seeing, and to be prepared to talk about this with a group or the class.

Unit 20: Non-fiction (information text): 'Chocolate: From bean to bar'

Overview

English curriculum objectives

- Listen to and discuss a wide range of fiction, poetry, plays, non-fiction and reference books or textbooks
- Read books that are structured in different ways and reading for a range of purposes
- Use dictionaries to check the meanings of words they have read
- Identify themes and conventions in a wide range of books
- Discuss words and phrases that capture the reader's interest and imagination
- Check that the text makes sense to them, discussing their understanding and explaining the meaning of words in context
- Ask questions to improve their understanding of a text
- Draw inferences such as inferring characters' feelings, thoughts and motives from their actions, and justifying inferences with evidence
- Predict what might happen from details stated and implied
- Identify main ideas drawn from more than one paragraph and summarise these
- Identify how language, structure and presentation contribute to meaning
- Retrieve and record information from non-fiction
- Participate in discussion about both books that are read to them and those they can read for themselves, taking turns and listening to what others say

Treasure House resources

- Comprehension Skills Pupil Book 3, Unit 20, pages 64–66
- Photocopiable Unit 20, Resource 1: True or false? page 103
- Photocopiable Unit 20, Resource 2: Food fact file, page 104

Additional resources

- Dictionaries or the internet (optional)
- *Chocolate: From bean to bar* by Anita Ganeri, whole text (optional)
- Other non-fiction texts about food products (optional)

Introduction

Teaching overview

Chocolate: From bean to bar is a non-fiction information text. It presents factual information about the origins of chocolate in Central America over 1,000 years ago, and its transition to Europe in the 16th century. The children are able to explore how language, structure and presentation contribute to meaning. The text features subheadings, simple paragraphs and a 'Did you know?' fact box.

Introduce the extract

Ask the children what they know about how chocolate is made, and invite them to share their knowledge with the class.

Tell the children that, in this lesson, they will focus on an extract from an information book about chocolate. Then they will answer questions about it. Remind them that sometimes they will find the answers to the questions written clearly in the extract, but that sometimes they may need to think a little harder and use their own ideas, supported by the text.

Ask the children to read the extract individually or in pairs. Ask them to note down any words they do not understand. Discuss any unknown or unusual vocabulary before setting the children to work answering the questions in the Pupil Book. Try to avoid discussing the content of the extract until after the children have answered the questions.

Pupil practice

Pupil Book pages 64–66

Get started

The children copy the sentences and complete them using information from the text.

Answers

1. The first people to grow <u>cacao</u> trees were the Maya people [1 mark]

2. The Maya and the Aztecs, who also lived in Central America, made a drink from the beans which they called <u>*chocolatl*</u>. [1 mark]

3. It was very bitter, and not much like <u>modern</u> chocolate drinks. [1 mark]

4. The Aztec ruler, Moctezuma, <u>collected</u> beans as taxes. [1 mark]

5. In the 16th century, Spanish explorers began to <u>conquer</u> Central America. [1 mark]

Try these

Assist the children if they ask for help with vocabulary, first discussing what they think the words might mean. Ask them to write sentences to answer the questions, explaining their answers with reference to the text or their own experiences.

Suggested answers

1. *The Maya people were the first people to grow cacao trees.* [example]

2. The Maya people lived in Central America more than 1,000 years ago. [2 marks]

3. The two terms used are 'cacao' and 'cocoa beans'. [1 mark]

4. I think they didn't add sugar because they didn't have any sugar. / I think they didn't add sugar because they liked the bitter taste. [1 mark]

5. I think they used cocoa beans as money because they were small / there were lots available / they were valuable. [1 mark]

Now try these

Open-ended questions

1. Sentences should be from an Aztec child's point of view, reacting to seeing Spanish explorers tasting *chocolatl* for the first time, and perhaps to them finding it bitter and/or adding sugar. [3 marks max]

2. Answers should recognise that the Spanish explorers took chocolate back to Spain (Europe) with them, and could add other details from the text or the children's imagination. [3 marks max]

3. Pictures should be relevant to the extract, including details it mentions. They should depict Spanish explorers tasting or looking at cocoa beans or *chocolatl*. Sentences should suggest a plausible reaction from an explorer. [3 marks max]

Support, embed & challenge

Support

Use Unit 20 Resource 1: True or false? to support the children in practising their reading memory skills. Ask them to try answering the questions without rereading the extract to find the answers. Then, when they have attempted the questions, they could use rereading to check their answers. (**Answers** True, False, True, True, False, False, True, False, True, True)

Embed

Use Unit 20 Resource 2: Food fact file to encourage the children to plan their own reports about a food of their choice. Enable the children to research facts about their chosen product and remind them to look back at the extract for guidance with the features, content and style of their reports.

Challenge

Ask groups to find out more about chocolate and how it developed, using library books or the internet. If possible, provide the full text of *Chocolate: From bean to bar* afterwards.

Homework / Additional activities

Drink diagram

Ask the children to research and draw a diagram of how a drink product is sourced or made. Ask them to add labels and a sentence describing what the process is.

Review unit 3: Poetry: 'The Green Hedgehog'   Pupil Book pages 67–68

Get started

Answers

The children copy the sentences and complete them using information from the poem.

1. I had a little <u>hedgehog</u>. [1 mark]

2. Its eyes were <u>closed</u> so tightly [1 mark]

3. It <u>seemed</u> to have just lumps and bumps [1 mark]

4. I took my hedgehog to the <u>vets</u> [1 mark]

5. The vets <u>took</u> just one look at it [1 mark]

Try these

Assist the children if they ask for help with vocabulary, first discussing what they think the words might mean. Ask them to write sentences to answer the questions, explaining their answers with reference to the text or their own experiences.

Suggested answers

1. *This poem is about a hedgehog.* [example]

2. The 'hedgehog' was really a cactus. [1 mark]

3. The speaker was afraid the 'hedgehog' might be dead because it was green, had spines that were thin and pale, sat completely still and had its eyes shut tightly. [2 marks]

4. Hedgehogs and cacti are similar as they both have spines (and are roundish in shape). [1 mark]

5. The vets felt uninterested in the 'hedgehog' as they look after animals, and it wasn't an animal. [2 marks]

Now try these

Open-ended questions

1. Sentences should be from the speaker's point of view, reacting to the news that the 'hedgehog' is actually a cactus. [3 marks max]

2. Rhyming words: 'ill'/'still', 'see'/'be', 'dead'/'said', '(attract) us'/'cactus'. The two new pairs of lines about the 'hedgehog' should rhyme. [3 marks max]

3. Pictures and labels should be relevant to the poem, including details it mentions. [3 marks max]

Ordering events

Complete the sentences to show the order in which things happened. Use the extract to help you.

First, the guests gathered around…
Next, the guests sang…
After that, Mr Oldcastle said…
Finally, they saw…

A thank-you letter

Write a letter from Mr Oldcastle to his guests, thanking them for coming to celebrate Gumdrop's birthday. Use the sentence starters below.

Dear friends,

Thank you for coming to…

I really enjoyed…

It was a shame that…

I hope you enjoyed…

From your friend,
Mr Oldcastle

Similes

A simile compares one thing to another thing. Similes usually use 'as' or 'like' to compare the two things.

For example: 'Painted as bright as a circus clown'.

Draw lines to complete the similes by making good comparisons.

as slow as…	ice
as cold as…	a kitten
as busy as…	sugar
as blind as…	a bat
as light as…	a pancake
as bright as…	a snail
as sweet as…	iron
as playful as…	the sun
as flat as…	a feather
as hard as…	a bee

My caterpillars poem

Continue the poem by writing more about the caterpillars.
Use four pairs of rhyming lines, as the 'Caterpillars'
poem does. Try to use one new simile in your poem.

Simile ideas
as smooth as silk
as bristly as a toothbrush
as hungry as a horse
as green as grass

My ideas for rhyming words

Caterpillars

By _____

_____

_____

_____

_____

_____

_____

_____

Comparing animals

Fill in the chart below with information about the cow.
Then choose two different animals and complete the chart.

Animal:	Cow		
How does it look?			
How do you feel about it?			
Where does it live?			
What does it do?			

My animal poem

Write your own poem about an animal of your choice.
Use at least eight lines.

As an extra challenge, try to include some rhyming words in the same pattern as in 'The Cow'. You could use the structure below.

Line 1: Describe the animal.
Line 2: Say how you feel about it.
Line 3: Say why you feel this way. You could rhyme this with Line 1.
Line 4: Add more detail about your reasons. You could rhyme this with Line 2.
Lines 5-8: Describe where the animal lives and what it does. You could try to use the same rhyme structure.

_____

By _____

1. _____

2. _____

3. _____

4. _____

5. _____

6. _____

7. _____

8. _____

Find the facts

Fill in the chart by finding the information in the 'Cheeky chimps' report. The first section has been done for you.

What happened?	*Monkeys escaped from a lorry.*
When did it happen?	
Where did it happen?	
Why did it happen?	
How did it happen?	
Who was involved?	
How did they feel?	
What did they say?	

A new news report

Write your own news report about an animal escaping from the zoo. Remember to give details that describe what happened, when, where, why and to whom.

THE DAILY NEWS

By

Retell the tale

Complete the sentences and add pictures to retell the tale of Thunder and Lightning.

1. Thunder and Lightning were two grumpy old sheep. They would always…	**2.** The villagers…
3. In the end, the village chief decided…	**4.** However, even from the sky…

The tale of Rain

Think about the way the two sheep in the story are like the thunder and lightning we hear and see in the sky.

Think about how a folk tale might explain rain as something made by a naughty elephant.

Write a short tale of your own about a naughty elephant called Rain.

How was Rain the elephant like rain that falls from the sky?
Where did Rain live?
How did she behave?
How did local people feel about her?
How and why does Rain get into the sky?

Now write your tale!

Making decisions

Think about the decisions made by the lion and
the mouse. How might things have worked out differently?

The lion

What did the lion decide to do?	
Why did he make that decision?	
What would have happened if he had made a different decision?	

The mouse

What did the mouse decide to do?	
Why did he make that decision?	
What would have happened if he had made a different decision?	

Another moral tale

Write another story with the same message ('Don't belittle little things'), using different animal characters.

You could write about a shark and a little squid. How can the little squid convince the shark to value him?

What animals will be in your tale?

How will they meet?

What decision will the bigger animal make?

How do they feel about each other, at this point?

How does the bigger animal learn to value the smaller one?

Before and after

Compare Duncan's life before and after he caught a cold by using the extract and your imagination to complete the table.

	Before catching a cold	After catching a cold
How do you think Duncan felt?		
What things could Duncan do?		
How did his friends and family treat him?		

How Duncan caught a cold

How did Duncan catch his cold? Use the extract and your imagination to write what happened before the children found him.

Use the template prompts to help you.

Duncan was a…
One day, he woke up feeling…
Later that day, he tried to light his fire…
Duncan's family and friends said…

Asking questions

Imagine you are Annie, Tim or Jenny. You have just read and reread the letter from Gran. What questions could you ask her about the move and about the new house?

Questions about the moving process	Questions about the new house
How many boxes did you need to pack?	What colour are the kitchen walls?

A letter home

Imagine you are Annie, Tim or Jenny. You are visiting Gran in the holidays. Use the template below to write a letter home to Mum and Dad, telling them about the new house and about your visit.

Seaview
Cliff Lane
Sandy Bay
SY13 7AB

Date: _____

Dear Mum and Dad,

We are having a great time at Gran's new house. The house is...

Today, we...

Tomorrow, we will...

I feel...

Love from

Annie, Tim and Jenny xxx

Quick quiz

How well have you explored the text? Use this quiz to find out. Use the text to help you find the answers.

What is the text about?	
Into how many sections is the text divided?	
How can you tell when a different section begins?	
What are the different sections about?	
How many different types of ants are described?	
How many individual facts can you find in the text?	
What do you think the text should also have included? Try to think of three things.	

Insect fact file

Make a fact file about another insect. Use subheadings, diagrams and lots of facts to make your fact file interesting for a reader.

First, plan your fact file.

Insect I will write about:

Ideas for diagrams:

Ideas for subheadings:

A letter of complaint

Imagine you are a guest at Sandy Bay Holiday Park.
You are very annoyed!

Firstly, choose why you are annoyed:

• The rules on the leaflet are too strict. You want to play your music loudly. You want to swim in the pool at night. This is supposed to be a fun holiday!

Or

• The guests in the caravan next to yours are breaking all the rules. The noise at night is driving you crazy!

Write a letter of complaint to the manager of Sandy Bay, explaining why you are so cross. Refer to the rules in the leaflet.

Dear Manager,

I am writing to complain about _____

_____

_____

_____

_____

_____

_____

Yours faithfully,

Information pack

Design an information pack for visitors to a new holiday park by planning two leaflets. For example:

- Things you must try

- Park rules

- Important information for visitors

The planning grid suggests features to include. You could also add your own ideas.

	Leaflet 1	Leaflet 2
Heading		
Subheadings		
An information paragraph		
Bullet-point information (rules, advice or directions)		
A diagram, map or pictures		
Special offers		

The bike competition

Read this story extract about the bike competition. Find and mark the information that matches the details provided on the poster.

Can you work out how old Jenny is?

The Bike Competition

Jenny woke up bright and early on Saturday morning. She felt so excited – she was surprised she had slept at all! She bounced down the stairs and checked the date on the calendar. It was Saturday 25th October. The date had a big red circle drawn around it.

Just then, Mum came into the kitchen. "Good morning, Jenny! Make sure you have a good breakfast today."

"I will, Mum," mumbled Jenny, her mouth already full of cereal.

Then Tom, Jenny's five-year-old brother, ran into the room. "And me! I need a good breakfast too! I'm ready to go. I've got my bike helmet ready, and my lucky trainers."

"You can't enter the race, Tom – you're too young," said Jenny.

"It's OK, Tom," Mum reassured him. "You can ride around the path while we watch Jenny in the race."

An hour later, at 9.30 a.m., they arrived at Crossfield Farm. Jenny had planned plenty of time to get ready for her race at 10 a.m. This was the last year that she would be able to enter the Juniors' race – next year, she'd be one of the Seniors!

Mum paid £2.00 for her and Tom's entry to watch the race, and then they made their way over to the refreshment tent to get some tea and squash. Tom also had a big chocolate chip cookie. Jenny saw her friends from the bike club, so she went off with them to prepare for the start of the race.

Jenny's heart was beating hard as she lined up at the start of the race. She had been practising for this for months, and she really hoped to finish in the top three. Suddenly the starting pistol popped – and they were off!

New event poster

Plan your own poster to advertise an event, such as a swimming competition or a school summer fair. Use this planning grid to help you think about what to include.

Name of event:	
Explanation of event:	
Location:	
Date:	
Time:	
People or animals involved:	
Any people or animals not permitted:	
Cost of tickets:	
How to buy tickets:	
What people need to bring:	
Other information:	

Rhyming words

Find the pairs of words in the poem that rhyme with the words in the bubbles. Write each pair in the correct bubble. Then add more rhyming words to each list. Can you fill the bubbles?

pies

fish

please

fed

weep

soot

stomp

frog

A new pet poem

Use this planning grid to help you write your own funny pet poem, in a style similar to that of 'Roger the Dog'. Write at least three pairs of rhyming lines and at least one comparison.

Pet I will write about
How the pet behaves
What the pet likes to do
What the pet likes to eat
Ideas for rhyming words
Things to which I could compare the pet

What was Peter thinking?

Add your ideas to this table to show what you imagine Peter would have been thinking at each part of the tale.

What was happening in the tale	What Peter was thinking
Peter lived with his family. He was always a problem for his mother, causing trouble and getting into scrapes.	
Mrs. Rabbit said that the rabbits could play in the field or down the lane, but not in Mr. McGregor's garden.	
"Your father had an accident there," said Mrs. Rabbit. "He was put into a pie by Mrs. McGregor."	
Flopsy, Mopsy and Cotton-tail went to gather blackberries, but Peter went into Mr. McGregor's garden.	
Peter ate some lettuces, French beans, radishes and parsley.	
Then Peter met Mr. McGregor. Mr. McGregor jumped up and ran after Peter!	

Peter in trouble

The extract says that Peter 'was always a problem for his mother, causing trouble and getting into scrapes'. Use the planning grid below to help you write about an earlier time that Peter caused trouble.

What is Peter doing at the beginning of your tale? Where is he? Who is he with?
What tempts Peter to go somewhere he shouldn't?
What happens to Peter? How does he get into trouble?
How does Peter get out of the dangerous situation? Who helps him?
What does Old Mrs. Rabbit say to Peter afterwards? How does Peter respond?

A 'proper' owl

Plop and the girl are not always the way they are expected to be. For example, Plop says girls don't have tails – but the girl he meets has a ponytail!

Fill in the chart to show what is expected of Plop and how he really is.

What is expected	How things really are
Owls like the dark	
	Plop goes "Eeeeek"
Owls can fly and land easily	
	Plop is huffy
	The girl has a ponytail

What happens next?

Write the next part of Plop's attempts to find out about the dark, when he goes into the woods and meets another person or animal.

Use the planning grid to order your thoughts.

Who will Plop meet in the woods?	
How will this person or animal first respond to Plop?	
What questions will Plop ask?	
How will the person or animal explain the dark?	
How will he feel?	
How will the scene end?	

True or false?

How carefully did you read the text? Check your memory by ticking 'true' or 'false' for each statement.

		true	false
1.	Many frogs have short tongues.	☐	☐
2.	Frogs shoot their tongues out to catch food.	☐	☐
2.	Vultures don't kill animals.	☐	☐
4.	Vultures hide in a hole waiting for an animal to die.	☐	☐
5.	Venus flytraps do not eat insects.	☐	☐
6.	A Venus flytrap closes up its leaves to trap an insect.	☐	☐
7.	When the insect dies, the Venus flytrap can digest it.	☐	☐
8.	Plants do not live off other plants.	☐	☐
9.	A parasite can be a plant or an animal.	☐	☐
10.	A parasite lives off another living thing without killing it.	☐	☐
11.	Venus flytraps are parasites.	☐	☐
12.	Fleas are parasites.	☐	☐

Information leaflet

Use the facts in the text to make your own information leaflet on 'funny feeders'. Use subheadings, diagrams and other features to make your fact file interesting for a reader. You could add extra information that you find out from the internet or library books.

Make notes on your extra research here:

| |
| |

Use this planning grid to make notes about what you will include.

| **Heading:** |
| **Subheading 1:** |
| **Facts to include:** |
| **Subheading 2:** |
| **Facts to include:** |
| **Subheading 3:** |
| **Facts to include:** |
| **Diagrams and images to include:** |

The car-trip story

Use this template and the poem to turn the events in the car into a short story. You could also add details using your imagination.

One day, Mum said, "Get packed up and ready to go. We are going on a car trip to…

The children eventually started to put their belongings into the car ready to go…

Mum turned the key and the engine roared into action. Mum turned to the children and said…

They had been in the car for half an hour, and the children were feeling restless…

Mum's view

Imagine that Mum is chatting to her friend on the telephone. Retell the events in the poem from Mum's point of view.

Finding the features

Label the start of the playscript with the features below.

The character speaking	The title of the play	Stage directions	Character speech

The Gigantic Turnip Tug

Narrator 1:   Once upon a time, a little old man and a little old woman …

Narrator 2:   Lived in a tiny farmhouse near an overgrown garden.

Narrator 3:   One morning they left the farmhouse and said …

(The Old Man and Old Woman walk to the garden bed.)

Old Woman: On such a fine spring morning …

Old Man: It's time to plant some vegetables in our garden!

Costumes and setting

Think about how the play scene should look. Use the grid below to note down costume ideas for each character, all the props needed and ideas about how the stage should look.

Costume ideas	
The narrators:	
The old man:	
The old woman:	
Props needed	
Stage set ideas	

Helga's character

Use the text and your own ideas to create a character profile of Helga, the children's stepmother.

Picture	Name
	Age
Physical description	**Personality**
Likes	**Dislikes**

Two diaries

Describe the events in the extract from the points of view of two of the characters: Hansel and Dad. Write a short paragraph for each diary.

Hansel's diary:

Dad's diary:

Romans and Egyptians

The extract mentions the Romans and Egyptian mummies. Read the information below to understand what Spider's class is studying.

The Romans
The ancient Romans were people who lived in Rome, a city in the centre of Italy. The city settlement has existed for over 2,750 years. The Romans were great warriors. Around 2,000 years ago, they had built a huge empire made up of the many countries they had invaded and conquered in battle. One of the countries they invaded was Britain. They were led by a famous emperor called Julius Caesar. Many Romans moved to Britain, and the Roman culture had a great impact on British life. What the Romans gave us • Language   • the calendar   • our legal system • central heating   • straight roads

The Egyptians
The ancient Egyptians were people who lived in Egypt, a country in Africa. Their settlements along the banks of the River Nile have existed for over 7,000 years. The Egyptians made very early progress in farming, medicine, politics and building. Ancient Egypt's most impressive buildings are still standing today. They are giant pyramids built to bury their leaders, who were called pharaohs, after they died. Before a pharaoh was buried, he was turned into a mummy: • His liver, lungs, intestines and stomach were put into jars. • His heart was cleaned and put back in his body. • His brain was pulled out on a hook through his nose, and then thrown away. • Then his body was dried out using salt, and stuffed with spices and rags. • After that, it was wrapped up in bandages and placed in a beautiful coffin.

Spider's character

Use the text and your own ideas to create a character profile of Spider.

Picture	Name
	Age
Physical description	**Personality**
Likes	**Dislikes**

True or false?

How carefully did you read the text? Check your memory by ticking 'true' or 'false' for each statement.

		true	false
1.	The Maya people were the first people to grow cacao trees.	☐	☐
2.	The Maya lived in London 100 years ago.	☐	☐
3.	The Maya called the beans 'cacao'.	☐	☐
4.	The Maya and the Aztecs made the beans into a drink.	☐	☐
5.	'Chocolatl' was naturally very sweet.	☐	☐
6.	Spanish explorers used the beans as money.	☐	☐
7.	Three beans could buy you an avocado.	☐	☐
8.	10 beans could buy you a turkey.	☐	☐
9.	Moctezuma was an Aztec ruler.	☐	☐
10.	People living in Europe didn't know about chocolate until the 16th century or later.	☐	☐

Food fact file

Make notes to write your own fact file about a food product.

I will write about:
When was it first discovered or invented?
From which country did it first come?
How has it changed to become the product we buy in the shops?
Why do people like it so much?
Other interesting facts
Images to include